Prepare for Zomb
Survive a Flooc

Also by Michael Walton
and from McFarland

The Horror Comic Never Dies: A Grisly History (2019)

Prepare for Zombies, Survive a Flood

Natural Disaster Lessons from Undead Cinema

MICHAEL WALTON

McFarland & Company, Inc., Publishers
Jefferson, North Carolina

Library of Congress Cataloguing-in-Publication Data

Names: Walton, Michael, 1970– author.
Title: Prepare for zombies, survive a flood : natural disaster lessons from undead cinema / Michael Walton.
Description: Jefferson, North Carolina : McFarland & Company, Inc., Publishers, 2023. | Includes index.
Identifiers: LCCN 2023043828 | ISBN 9781476693866 (paperback : acid free paper) ♾
ISBN 9781476651576 (ebook)
Subjects: LCSH: Emergency management. | Zombie films—History and criticism. | BISAC: PERFORMING ARTS / Film / Genres / Horror | SOCIAL SCIENCE / Disasters & Disaster Relief | LCGFT: Film criticism.
Classification: LCC HV551.2 W345 2023 | DDC 363.34/8—dc23/eng/20231016
LC record available at https://lccn.loc.gov/2023043828

British Library cataloguing data are available

ISBN (print) 978-1-4766-9386-6
ISBN (ebook) 978-1-4766-5157-6

Printed in the United States of America

McFarland & Company, Inc., Publishers
Box 611, Jefferson, North Carolina 28640
www.mcfarlandpub.com

Table of Contents

Preface

This particular book has been a long time in the making—whether I originally knew it or not.

I grew up in a very rural area in southwestern Virginia. The town that I lived in was so deeply set into the hills and valleys of the Appalachian Mountains that we all learned a certain amount of survival skills and the importance of self-sufficiency regardless of if you chose to or not. The local fire department (and so all EMTs) was staffed by volunteers. This is not to say that these volunteers didn't do the job to the best of their ability, because nothing would be further from the truth. These were as dedicated a group of individuals as you could ever hope to meet (especially considering they were doing this very tough job for free), but they all had full-time paying jobs and other responsibilities.

The idea of a fire hall that was staffed 24/7 by a group of people just waiting to be dispatched somewhere was a completely alien prospect to my community. That was something we just saw on television. If you called 9-1-1 and needed help, the First Responders would many times have to be called away from their jobs in order to respond to the call. They would have to leave their jobs, make their way to the station, and then answer the call. The overall ruralness of the area also created extra difficulties. I recall my parents calling the police one time and waiting nearly half an hour for the police to find our house. Houses were few and far between and they sat in hidden hollows or down unmarked (and many times unpaved) roads so they were not always very easy to find—even if you knew where you were going.

Being that far away from "civilization" presented other challenges as well. A close friend of mine had the distinction of growing up in a house that was the last house on the line for all major utilities. When there was a service interruption, their house was the absolute last one to get the service restored. A storm with strong winds could have them without power for several days at a time. Telephone service (these are pre-cellphone days) could easily be out for several weeks. During all this, they were naturally expected to go to their jobs and get the kids to school. Normal day-to-day life had to continue whether you had power, heat, or running water in your house or not. As you can imagine, this lifestyle taught you to maintain a certain level of self-sufficiency. You couldn't rely on the fact that modern conveniences like heat, power, water, and communications would always be readily available. When these services were interrupted, you also couldn't count on them being restored in a timely fashion.

Later in life, I moved away from rural Virginia into a more populated area. Now I live in a place where widespread power outages are so infrequent that they make the news when they happen. Emergency services are staffed by paid professionals and should I ever need to call 9-1-1, I can expect a response in minutes. *Minutes!* It is a drastic change from how I grew up, but certain skills are never really unlearned. It is still interesting to watch people "panic buy" at the threat of severe weather. The first thing that goes through my mind is the fact that you should always have several days' worth of food and supplies on hand in case of an emergency so there is never a need to panic buy. Plus, what do people typically panic buy? I've watched people stock up on milk, bread, and eggs right before a snowstorm is forecast to hit us. I'm not sure what makes an impending blizzard make people crave French toast, but maybe my mind works differently.

As a way to give back to my community, I started volunteering with my local Community Emergency Response Team (CERT). A CERT is an all-volunteer force of local residents who are trained in disaster response skills, first aid, and light search and rescue operations. It is designed to support emergency response teams so that they can be freed up to do their highly skilled work where they are most needed. Another of the responsibilities of our CERT is to help educate the public on fire safety and disaster preparedness. September is National Preparedness Month, so there are usually plenty of opportunities for us to hold presentations and speak with community members.

Doing this led me to realize how different my upbringing was from many other people. The average person is not well prepared for a natural disaster. Surveys have shown that at least 60 percent of people have no emergency preparedness plan in place at all. They either think that the process is too hard, that it is too expensive, or (possibly the worst of all), that they don't need one because something like that would never happen to them.

By now, you're probably thinking "Where do the zombies come in?" We're getting there now.

I am an avid horror movie fan and I am a huge fan of the zombie movie genre. I have probably seen every zombie movie ever made (much to the chagrin of my wife). If you know any fans of zombie movies (or are one yourself), then you know that everyone who has seen even one zombie movie always has their own plan for what they would do in the situation. It can be as small as *Night of the Living Dead* where the zombie invasion started one evening and was contained the next day or as widespread as *The Walking Dead* where the zombies have taken over and society has collapsed—but they're going to have a plan of some kind. They will have ideas on where to go to be safe, on how to defend themselves, on how to find food.

That's a lot of thought that is put into planning for a purely fictional situation. What's more telling is all of the people who have fully fleshed-out Zombie Apocalypse Survival Plans, but don't have a radio or batteries for their flashlight in case of a real disaster. There should be some way to conflate the two ideas.

Hence the birth of this book. I know many people are woefully unprepared for a natural disaster. I also know that there are many great books on disaster preparedness, but most of the time those books only target an audience that is already prepared. Remember, the typical mindset is that a natural disaster won't happen to me so why would I go out and get a book about something that I don't think is a problem?

I created this book to draw in a different segment of the population. This book is geared for people who would never read a book on disaster preparedness guide but who love a good zombie movie. It only stands to reason that if you can put enough thought into a plan for surviving the Zombie Apocalypse (which will never happen), then you can use those same skills to put together a plan to help your family comfortably survive a natural disaster (which is very likely to happen). If you look at the primary goals of any character in a zombie movie, their motivations are practically identical to someone surviving a natural disaster. They get themselves to safety. They seek out shelter. They communicate with the outside world—either to find news of what is happening or to contact their friends and family, or both. If the situation goes on long enough, they locate a sufficient supply of food and water.

That is why this book exists to educate people on how to prepare themselves for a completely fictional event. After all, what is the worst thing that can happen? Suppose you go through all of the steps to get ready for the Zombie Apocalypse, but you end up using that preparedness to allow you to comfortably ride out a natural disaster. Were your efforts wasted?

This book is written to help people be ready for an event that is limited in scope—meaning your services may be interrupted but eventually they will be restored. Many books referencing the Zombie Apocalypse are written from the perspective that society as a whole has collapsed and will never return to its former state. This book does not take that stance. A disaster may strike where you live and it may be cataclysmic in nature. The damage could be widespread and severe but, despite how it may feel, this will not be the end of the world. Work will begin almost immediately after the disaster to get things back to normal. Roads will be cleared, infrastructure will be rebuilt, utilities will be restored, and damage to structures will be repaired.

It may take weeks for your daily life to truly get back to "normal," but normality will return. This book is written from that perspective. Nowhere in this book will I advise anyone to build bomb shelters, stockpile years' worth of food, store precious metals, or move to the country and start a farm. You may have to live "off the grid" for a little bit until your utilities are restored, but they will be restored. It is very common for books like this to take that "prepper" mentality and have readers planning for the collapse of modern society, but that is not my goal.

This book is designed to give the reader a calm, rational, and level-headed approach to preparing themselves and their families for some of the worst things that can happen. Natural disasters are not fun to experience, but having some basic readiness can make the experience at least a little more comfortable and a little less stressful. As you make preparations and build a mindset of readiness, you will find that it provides you a great deal of comfort knowing that you are now prepared for the unexpected. Let's face it, if you can prepare to survive the Zombie Apocalypse, then you can certainly survive a "mere" natural disaster!

Introduction

This book is a practical, "real world" guide to how you, the reader, can prepare yourself and your family to survive the Zombie Apocalypse.

Just to make sure we are all on the same page, the Zombie Apocalypse is a near-extinction level event in which dead human corpses are reanimated through some unknown or unexplained event. These newly reanimated corpses are mobile (even though in a somewhat limited capacity) and driven by only one instinct—to feed on the flesh (and more specifically the brains) of the living. A person killed by a zombie will naturally reanimate as a zombie themselves with the same all-consuming hunger for living flesh.

A person bitten (or in some cases even scratched) by a zombie will inevitably fall victim to an infection. Flu-like symptoms will quickly develop followed by a raging fever, weakness, and disorientation. The infection is almost 100 percent fatal and kills its victim in a matter of hours. The victim then, of course, reanimates as a zombie.

The Zombie Plague spreads very quickly. Local police forces are overwhelmed and cities become charnel houses. The military is mobilized, but by this time they are significantly outnumbered by the living dead. They fight bravely and even make limited progress, but they are ultimately overrun and consumed. Vast numbers from the population of the world as we know it are killed in a matter of weeks. Governments dissolve and nations cease to exist. Modern life as we know it comes to an abrupt end. Power grids fail, plunging the world into an unending blackout. Billions of people are dead and most of those billions of people now roam the earth looking to destroy any last surviving remnants of humanity.

This is the point for which you, the fearless reader, are trying to prepare. You want to ensure that you and your family survive. How is that possible?

The answer to this is amazingly simple—you don't have to worry about it. It's not going to happen. The Zombie Apocalypse is a plot device used in horror movies and books and has absolutely no basis in the real world.

Dead bodies do not just get back up and start moving around. Even if they did, modern burials have very strict guidelines. A body is sealed in a sturdy coffin which is then placed in a concrete vault which is in turn buried several feet underground. This means that the buried dead are not very likely to trouble anyone. The recently deceased would hardly be any more trouble, either.

Assuming there could be some type of virus that had the ability to restart a dead brain and central nervous system—even in a limited capacity, the body would still be a collection of formerly living organic tissue and thus would be subject to decay. The process of decay starts immediately after the cessation of life and progresses at a steady pace (hastened or slowed by environmental conditions) until the body is completely decomposed. In a temperate climate, it is not unreasonable to assume that a zombie's body would decay to the point that its mobility would be severely limited within a period of days to weeks.

This decomposition process obviously affects all of the muscles and tissue so it also stands to reason that a zombie's ability to bite or claw anything would be reduced rapidly as well. Simply put, a zombie might have the ability to injure or kill a human for just a few short days before its body decays to the point that its muscles would no longer be able to move it around. It would then remain a barely mobile mass of rotting flesh for a week or two until all of the remaining flesh, tissue, and organs liquified away. Even in large numbers, this hardly seems like a very effective threat.

Couple this with the fact that there are no known viruses in existence today that have the ability to spread as quickly as the Zombie Plague Virus would have to. Generally in movies, a person is shown being bitten by a zombie and the unfortunate victim begins to show signs of illness in just a few short hours. The time between a person's exposure to a virus and that person showing the first symptoms of infection is known as the *incubation period.*

No known virus has such a short incubation period. The common cold, one of the fastest spreading and most rampant viruses, has an incubation period of between 24 and 72 hours. Even truly terrifying viruses like Ebola have an incubation period of 2 to 21 days—with an average incubation period of 8 to 10 days. The bubonic plague, the virus responsible for killing one-third of the population of Europe in the 14th century, has an incubation period of two to six days. As deadly as Ebola and the bubonic plague are they pale in comparison to the Zombie

Plague Virus. Ebola has killed fewer than 10,000 people since its discovery in 1976. The bubonic plague still exists, but less than a dozen Americans each year are diagnosed with it—hardly the Black Death of the 14th century. This is, of course, due to modern medicine and the cleanliness of modern living conditions, since the plague is spread by the bites of fleas that live on rats and other vermin.

It is also perfectly reasonable to think that the American military would be up to the task of crushing an undead horde if they were ever called on to do so. The United States has roughly 1.3 million active troops with nearly another million in reserve. These troops are stationed at military bases throughout the United States and the world and are ready to mobilize at a moment's notice. If need be, the military could have "boots on the ground" in very short order.

The United States Army maintains a Quick Reaction Force (QRF) which is designed to have a company of troops (150 soldiers plus their command) anywhere in the world in 24 hours, a battalion (800 troops) anywhere in the world within 48 hours, and a brigade combat team (4,000) anywhere in the world within 72 hours. This rapid response would put the most highly trained and best equipped fighting force in the world in a position to engage the zombie horde within a matter of hours. Having seen how the U.S. military has accomplished things in the past, I would certainly favor them over a shambling mass of rotting zombies.

You would think that after systematically destroying the idea behind this book in the introduction that there wouldn't be anything left to write about. That's not quite true. Although the idea behind the Zombie Apocalypse is complete fiction, it has spawned countless movies and books—and for good reason. There are practical life lessons that can be gleaned from zombie movies. For example: the protagonists in every zombie movie tend to strive for the same series of goals.

- They want to get themselves out of harm's way
- They want to find some type of shelter in which they can be safe
- They attempt to communicate with the outside world to get more information on what is going on
- Realizing they will need to be self-reliant for a period of time, they need to find a source for food and water

All of us have watched zombie movies and put ourselves in the place of the survivors. "If I were in that situation," we would think, "what would I do?" "Would it be better to hunker down in that farmhouse or should I take a car and hit the road?" "Do I have access to food or should I raid that grocery store?" "Do I know if my family is safe?" "Is there a radio or television somewhere broadcasting news of what is going on?" These are all practical questions that anyone would ask in this type of situation. While we never have to worry about a Zombie Apocalypse, there are plenty of real world situations where a person could find themselves in a similar situation to a survivor in a zombie movie.

Natural disasters happen every day all across the world and regular people are forced to ask themselves some very similar sounding questions. Am I safe here? Can I find shelter? How do I communicate with my family? How do I get news about what is going on? Am I going to have enough food and water to make it through this?

Natural disasters come in all shapes and sizes and they affect people's lives in very different ways. Strong winds from a storm can knock down power lines putting communities into a blackout for hours or days at a time. Housefires can displace a family from their home. Wildfires can destroy entire neighborhoods in a matter of hours. Tornados, hurricanes, and earthquakes can also leave people without shelter, food, or access to clean water for days or even weeks at a time.

These are all devastating events and, unlike the Zombie Apocalypse, they are very real. Last year more than 25 million Americans were affected by a natural disaster of some sort. Unfortunately, studies have shown that only about 25 percent of American households have any type of disaster preparedness at all. Poor planning for a natural disaster could have dangerous or even fatal repercussions.

That brings us to the purpose of this book. In the coming chapters, I take the concept of preparing for a natural disaster and frame it in the thought exercise of preparing for the Zombie Apocalypse. The idea behind this is that after a natural disaster strikes, you will likely be left without the benefit of many of the conveniences of modern life (i.e., no power, no phone, no water, etc.). Just like the survivors in a zombie movie, it will be necessary for you to be self-sufficient (or very nearly so) until services have been restored. So how long should you be preparing for?

Natural disasters come in all shapes and sizes and they affect an area in different ways. A natural disaster's impact on your life for the purpose of this book will be classified by approximately how long it will take for utilities and other standard services to resume or, in other words, how long you should expect to be self-sufficient. I have broken these up into three categories:

- A small scale disaster with normal services returning within 24 to 72 hours—the Night of the Living Dead Scenario
- A more widespread disaster affecting a larger area when you

might be expected to be self-sufficient for two to three weeks—the 28 Days Later Scenario
- A catastrophic disaster affecting a large area. Damage is widespread and severe and you could potentially need to be self-sufficient for a month or longer—the Walking Dead Scenario

Having laid out that framework, I think it is important to specify what this book is not about. This book is not a "prepper's" guide. A "prepper" is someone who is preparing (aka prepping) for what they feel is the inevitable collapse of modern society. Preppers are preparing for an actual doomsday scenario in which everything we know as modern life (power, water, the Internet, governments, etc.) is destroyed and never returns. Preppers are planning on becoming self-sufficient and remaining that way for the rest of their natural lives. This book is written to help you prepare yourself and your family to be safe and comfortable in the event that a natural disaster temporarily interrupts your normal life. Nowhere in this book will I tell you to buy a farm far away from major cities, join a militia, or stockpile precious metals. I will present to you the information you need to comfortably, safely, and with the least amount of stress make it through a period of time (be it days or weeks) if you were temporarily without power, water, or other aspects of your daily life.

Chapter 1

Planning Ahead

The absolute worst time to begin planning your response to a natural disaster is right after the disaster has struck. By then, your ability to plan has been taken away and all you can do is respond. This is not an enviable position. Consider this: you are sitting at home watching television one evening. Your spouse is at work so you have the house to yourself and you're binge watching one of your guilty pleasure shows when suddenly you hear the wind pick up outside. Rain begins to fall, followed by loud crashes of thunder and bright flashes of lightning. This goes on for several minutes until suddenly everything goes dark. Your power is out and a glance out the window shows the power is out for your neighbors as well. What now? Was there severe weather in the forecast? Could there be even worse weather on the way? Can you even find your way around the house in the dark? Do you have flashlights? Batteries? Candles? A way to light the candles? You should report the power outage to your utility company, but do you know the number? What if the power is out for hours? What about all of the food in the fridge? Your spouse is at work. Is the power out for them as well? How can you contact them? What if the power is out all night? You have to go to work tomorrow. Will the garage door open without power? As you can imagine, sitting alone in the dark while a storm rages outside is not the best time to begin thinking about these types of questions. This is where a disaster plan comes into play.

What to Prepare for

A natural disaster cannot be prevented and it is impossible to accurately predict when and where a natural disaster will happen. Your goal is to be as prepared as possible for a volatile, unpredictable situation. While you can never predict **when** a disaster will strike, you can at least know **what types** of natural disasters are more apt to occur in your area of the country and modify your plans accordingly. Obviously things like house fires and power outages can happen to anyone anywhere. Different regions of the country have to take special care to prepare for the types of natural disasters that frequent that area. Areas along the Gulf Coast need to be prepared for hurricanes. Anyone living near an active fault line should be prepared for earthquakes. People living in the Central Plains states around "tornado alley" obviously need to plan for tornadoes. Northern states, while far away from earthquakes and hurricanes, have the extra complication of having to take into consideration the frigid winter weather that they get in those areas. Protection against the extreme cold must be a part of any Northerner's disaster plan in addition to any other disaster preparations that are made since exposure can be dangerous or even fatal if not properly prepared for.

Forewarned Is Forearmed

In the classic 1968 George Romero zombie movie *Night of the Living Dead*, brother and sister Johnny and Barbara are driving to a rural cemetery to visit their father's grave and place a wreath of flowers on it. As they arrive at the cemetery, the car radio, which had apparently been silent for a while, comes back on the air in what sounds like a frantic attempt to begin broadcasting again. Just as the words "Do not be alarmed" are being spoken, Johnny turns off the radio and gets out of the car. Barbara at this point is more concerned with finding their father's grave and Johnny just assumes that there was some minor glitch at the radio station that prevented them from broadcasting. As the movie goes on, of course, we learn that the radio broadcast was most likely going to be giving information regarding the strange attacks that have been taking place.

Johnny and Barbara, having been on a three hour drive to the cemetery, had no idea about the impending crisis that was unfolding around them. Had Johnny just listened to the radio broadcast for a little longer, things could have turned out drastically differently for him and Barbara—although George Romero would possibly have had a much shorter movie on his hands.

Being out of touch with one's surroundings in the real world could have serious consequences as well. Fortunately for us, modern society has several things in place which allow us to stay informed about potential natural disasters.

NOAA Weather Radio—This is an automated network of radio stations in the United States that broadcast weather information from a local National Weather Service office. These broadcasts happen 24 hours a day.

The concept behind the NOAA Weather Radio started out as an experiment. In 1960, the United States Weather Bureau began broadcasting marine weather information in Chicago and New York City on two radio stations. This proved to be valuable information for mariners and the shipping industry so the number of broadcasting stations and locations began to steadily increase. On April 11–12, 1965, a tornado outbreak ripped through Indiana, Ohio, Michigan, Wisconsin, Illinois, and Iowa: 47 tornadoes touched down, killing 271 people and injuring 1,500 in the second-biggest tornado outbreak on record at the time.

In the aftermath of that devastation, the United States Weather Bureau recommended the establishment of a nationwide radio network that could be used to broadcast weather warnings to the media, schools, public safety institutions, and the general public. The United States Weather Bureau's already growing network of maritime safety radio stations was the best candidate for this to become a reality and so the expansion of the radio network continued throughout the United States.

Control of the broadcast eventually came under the management of the National Oceanic and Atmospheric Administration (NOAA) and the system became known as the NOAA Weather Radio. Coverage was expanded to include coastal areas in the aftermath of Hurricane Camille which made landfall on August 17, 1969, as a Category 5 storm striking Bay St. Louis, Mississippi, killing 259 and causing $1.42 billion in damages ($9.7 billion in 2023 dollars).

NOAA Weather Radio operates over 1,000 radio stations and serves 95 percent of the U.S. population. It covers all 50 U.S. states and adjacent coastal waters, as well as the territories of Puerto Rico, the U.S. Virgin Islands, Guam, American Samoa, and Saipan. This NOAA system continually broadcasts local weather forecasts, climate summaries, and lake or coastal water forecasts (where applicable). During severe weather, the broadcast schedule is reduced to hazardous weather outlooks, short-term forecasts, special weather statements, and tropical weather summaries (where applicable). The NOAA Weather Radio is also connected with the FCC's Emergency Alert System and will occasionally broadcast non-weather related events such as national security statements and public safety statements (such as AMBER Alerts).

Dedicated weather radios as well as regular AM/FM radios with an additional weather radio receiver built-in are available for purchase online and in retail stores where consumer electronics are sold. They are generally very reasonably priced although the actual model and extra features included may increase the overall price. In any case, a NOAA Weather Radio is an invaluable tool in preparedness for natural disasters. No home should be without one (at least one) and preferably one that is powered by batteries.

Opt-In Text Notifications

Nowadays many of us are more likely to have our smartphone handy instead of a radio. Knowing this fact, many local communities have services in place to allow local public safety offices to send out information via text message. Check with your local city or town government offices or your local public safety offices. These services are typically an "opt-in" system, which means you are required to sign up in order to receive the notifications. These services are an excellent way to stay informed in the case of an emergency since text messages can be received anywhere there is cell phone signal coverage. This helps you to stay informed even when you are out of the house and away from the television and radio.

Enhanced Telephone Notification

While just about everyone has a cellphone, some people still prefer a traditional landline telephone. Emergency information is still available to traditional landlines as well. Many local communities have implemented an Enhanced Telephone Notification (ETN) system which can send an emergency notification via a phone call to a landline telephone—essentially like a "reverse 9-1-1" system. This can prove to be an invaluable service to at-risk individuals, the elderly, or anyone without ready access to a cell phone. You should contact your local public safety offices or emergency management offices to see if ETN is available in your area and, if not, what other options you have.

Smartphone Apps

Aside from making phone calls and sending and receiving text messages, smartphones can run a huge number of apps—some of which are very useful for disaster preparedness.

FEMA App—The Federal Emergency Management Agency (FEMA) has created a very useful and full-featured app. Using it you can receive weather service alerts, find tips for staying safe before, during, and after 20+ different types of hazards, and locate (and get directions to) FEMA shelters and disaster recovery centers. The FEMA app also lets you save a customized list of items in your family's Emergency Kit. In addition, the app allows you to take pictures of the disaster area with your cell phone and then submit them to a public map using a feature called Disaster Reporter. The FEMA app is available in English and Spanish and it is available for both Apple and Android phones.

American Red Cross Emergency App—The American Red Cross offers several different disaster preparedness apps. They have specific apps that provide alerts for tornadoes, hurricanes, and earthquakes, but their main app is the American Red Cross Emergency app. The Emergency app combines more than 35 different emergency alerts in one app and you can customize the alerts to show you the alerts most important to you. The alerts can also be customized to not only your current location, but the location where your friends and family live—a perfect way to help keep a loved one safe even if they are miles away. The Emergency app also provides information on safety during a flood, severe thunderstorm, hurricane, earthquake, wildfire, tornado, and several more natural disasters. It features information on how to react to weather emergencies that affect a large area—such as a mudslide or snowstorm.

The Emergency app provides directions to the closest Red Cross shelters. Possibly one of the best features of the app is the "Family Safe" feature. "Family Safe" allows you to instantly check on the safety of a loved one—even if they do not have the Emergency app. "Family Safe" lets you send a message to a friend or loved one. Their answers of "I'm safe" or "I'm not safe" will instantly come back to you. If they reply that they are not safe, their location is shown on a map and you can also call them. The Emergency app also has an "I'm safe" button which lets you assure your friends and family that you are not in danger.

Among the many apps that the American Red Cross offers, they have a very informative First Aid app which provides step-by-step instructions, videos, and animations for various basic first aid scenarios as well as a button to quickly call 9-1-1 and a hospital locator. The American Red Cross also provides a Pet First Aid app which has step-by-step instructions for over 25 different pet first aid situations.

All of the American Red Cross apps are available in English and Spanish for both Apple and Android phones.

The Weather Channel App—The Weather Channel also has an app. It is a more streamlined app than the ones previously mentioned. Focusing mainly on the weather (as one would expect), the Weather Channel app tracks weather and provides local forecasts. It also delivers alerts for severe weather. The Weather Channel app is available for both Apple and Android phones.

Civil Defense Sirens

Civil Defense sirens (or air raid sirens or tornado sirens) are large sirens located throughout many communities and sounded to provide warnings. Initially put in place during World War II to warn citizens about incoming air raids, they were repurposed after the end of the war to warn citizens about an incoming nuclear strike. Fortunately for everyone, they were never used for that purpose. Communities have since started using them to warn people about dangerous weather moving into the area—typically tornadoes. Some areas go further and will sound the sirens again when the dangerous weather has moved out of the region.

Other more rural areas have also been known to use the Civil Defense sirens as a signal to mobilize the volunteer fire department into action. If your community has Civil Defense sirens in it, find out from your local public safety office if they are still in use and, if so, what they are used for. Generally communities that use Civil Defense sirens for the purpose of warning their citizens will also test them on a regular basis—which is a great time to make sure you can hear them from your house or a local park where you spend time. My city, for example, tests their Civil Defense sirens at noon on the first Saturday of each month. It is also important to point out that Civil Defense sirens are only designed to act as a warning to people outside. Even though they are loud, they are significantly less noticeable if you are inside a building.

Local Notification Systems

While there is no substitute for keeping yourself informed, it is worth mentioning that many organizations (schools, workplaces, community centers, houses of worship) have their own emergency warnings. If you spend significant time in any of these places, you should familiarize yourself with their warning systems and what to do in case of an emergency or natural disaster.

Family Emergency Communication Plan

One of the most important points to keep in mind when planning for a natural disaster is that they tend to happen at very inconvenient times. A thorough disaster plan is great when everyone is safe at home, but how often does that really happen? People work away from home. Children go to school and college. Schedules are full and people are moving around a lot. Just like the outbreak of the Zombie Apocalypse always seems to happen at the worst possible time, a natural disaster is very likely to happen when you and your family are not together. What happens then? How can you be sure your loved ones are safe while assuring them that you are safe as well? Should everyone stay put or try to head home?

The answer to these questions is a good Family Emergency Communication Plan. Just as simple as it sounds, it is a plan in which you and your family will know how to establish some form of communication with each other in the event that you are separated during a natural disaster. Once you have established communication and made sure of everyone's safety, the Family Emergency Communication Plan also covers the "what's next" aspect. Clear instructions are in place for everyone so that they know when to go, where to go, how to get there, and what to do when they are there.

First and foremost, you will need to collect all contact information from your family. For each family member, you will want their name, cell phone number, any other phone numbers (landline, work phone, school, etc.), email address, any relevant social media account names, and any important medical information. Email addresses and social media information is important because a disaster could damage cell phone towers to the point they are unusable or simply overwhelmed by the volume of incoming calls. Even if you don't have cell phone service, you could still have access to the Internet which would allow you to make contact with someone using email or social media.

This information should be clearly printed on a card and every member of the family should have a copy of the card at all times in their wallet, purse, or backpack—something that they always have with them. Another copy of this information should be centrally located in your house. Obviously, this is not just for your family members—include your information as well. This is the first step to ensuring that everyone can communicate with everyone else.

Next, you should establish an out-of-town contact person and they should be given all of this information to act as a central point of contact if needed. It is not unheard of in a natural disaster for local phone lines to be overwhelmed or reduced in capacity whereas calls or texts out of the state still go through.

Here are some other quick points to remember:

- Every family member should have every other family member's emergency contact information in their cell phone.
- Every family member should have an ICE (In Case of Emergency) entry in their phone's contacts. This is used for first responders or hospital personnel to contact the next of kin of a cellphone's owner in order to obtain medical and support information. This assumes, of course, that the phone is working and not locked. ICE information can be added to the lock screen of a cell phone either by a setting on the phone itself or by certain apps. This is a very worthwhile thing to put in place. If you (or your family member) were found unconscious or unresponsive, having ICE information in a phone could help medical professionals as well as notifying the rest of your Family Emergency Plan group what has happened to that individual.
- Create a family group on everyone's phone contacts. The family group should have all of the family in it. This allows one message to go to the entire group at once instead of having to send multiple messages to multiple contacts. Quick communication is essential and this is a time-saver. A family group message will also prevent someone from accidentally being left out of an important communication. In a crisis, it is much easier to send one message to a group than to send multiple text messages to multiple people while trying to remember if you left anyone out.
- Designate a lead person. This person will have the final word as to where the remaining family members go. They will decide whether people should stay where they are or if they should head for a designated meeting place. A second lead person should be designated in case the primary lead person is incapacitated or otherwise unable to communicate. Having one person in charge ensures that everyone is on the same page and following the same set of instructions. This is vitally important to make sure a geographically separated group of people get to safety or remain safe.
- In an emergency a text message should be your first means of communication. When disaster strikes, local cell towers can very quickly become overwhelmed with calls. Depending on the nature of the emergency, cell towers could be damaged or destroyed, which will limit call capacity even further. Text messages are very small and require very little overhead to process so they can travel on a cell system with reduced capacity.
- Keep communications short and to the point. Regardless of what method of communication you use, in the middle of an

emergency is not the time to catch up on the news. You want to establish your safety and your location, so a text message like "I'm OK. At library" is optimal.

- Have everyone commit important numbers to memory. A contact in the phone is great, but what happens if your phone is damaged? Memorizing every person's number in your Family Emergency Plan might be asking a lot, but memorizing two or three key numbers is completely reasonable and could mean the difference between being able to communicate and being out of the loop.
- Don't forget about landlines as an option for communication. Remember a world before cell phones? People were still able to communicate with each other with regular old telephones—big clunky devices with cords that plugged into the wall. All facetiousness aside, a landline telephone can still be an important tool when communicating in an emergency. Cell phone towers are only designed to handle a certain call volume. On a regular day, the usage of a particular cell phone tower never reaches the saturation point where it can no longer process calls. In the aftermath of a natural disaster, you can't count on this being the case. Also consider the fact that cellphone towers could be damaged or possibly destroyed in a natural disaster making the ability to complete a cell phone call even more difficult. The public telephone infrastructure is huge and is designed with built-in redundancies, which means it can be a more reliable means of communication in the event of a widespread natural disaster.
- Any method of communication is a good one. While text messages, cellphones, and landline phone calls are a great way of communicating, don't limit yourself to just those methods. Most social media apps (Twitter, Instagram, Facebook) have the ability to directly communicate with an account holder. In the event of a large-scale disaster, Facebook also has a Crisis Response system by which you can mark yourself as Safe in a disaster area. You also have the ability to request information from your Facebook friends in a disaster area as to whether they are safe or not.
- Traditional email is also a viable alternative method of communication. While email doesn't provide the immediacy of text messaging or direct messaging through social media apps, it can still prove to be a useful communication tool. Whereas cell phone calls and text messages require a working

cellular network to successfully transmit, email messages are transmitted over the Internet. The Internet was designed to be resilient enough that an interruption of service in one geographical area would not have any overall effect on the Internet as a whole. This means that you could be in the middle of an area that has been devastated by a natural disaster and (provided you manage to find some type of Internet connection) still not be unable to communicate with your family and loved ones.

Family Emergency Meeting Place

Once you have successfully established communication with your family and loved ones and ascertained everyone's immediate safety, the next step is to determine if they are in a location that is likely to stay safe. Essentially, you need to decide whether you (or your family members) should stay where you are and hunker down or if you need to leave the area for someplace safer. In the case that you and your family are separated when a disaster strikes, part of your Family Emergency Communication Plan should include several Family Emergency Meeting Places. Different places should be chosen based on if your plans involve taking shelter in your house or whether you need to leave your house due to its becoming unsafe or being too damaged to provide proper shelter.

- Inside your house—if you plan on meeting in a safe place in your house, it should be the safest and sturdiest room in the house. This should be a small, interior windowless room on the lowest floor. Depending on the construction of your house, this could even be a closet or bathroom. An interior room with no windows will definitely hamper your ability to monitor what is going on outside, but this is by far the safest place. Many types of natural disasters are accompanied by high winds. Debris carried by these winds can shatter windows and cause serious injury to anyone close to them.
- Outside your house—Situations can occur that can suddenly make your house unsafe. The zombie horde could overcome your defenses and gain entry to your house. In a more practical scenario, a fire could break out causing you to have to suddenly evacuate. Strong winds could damage the roof of your house, leaving it unsuitable for occupancy. In any case, you should plan for a meeting place outside, but still in your

immediate neighborhood. This could be as simple as the edge of the driveway, a big tree in the cul-de-sac down the street, or even a neighbor's house.

- Outside your neighborhood—A widespread natural disaster could make it impossible to even get into your neighborhood. All roads going into your development could be blocked by downed trees or debris or rendered impassible by flood waters or blocked off by emergency personnel. You should establish a family meeting place that is located outside of your neighborhood for just such an event. This should be a place that is easily reachable and recognizable. Good examples of this type of meeting location would be the local public library, a community center, a house of worship, or a friend's house.
- Outside of your city—The Zombie Apocalypse is not going to happen at a convenient time. What if everything goes sideways while you're on vacation or visiting an out of town relative? A thorough plan should have contingencies in place to insure your family's safety even when you are outside of the familiar confines of your home town (or even your home state). These types of meeting places will need to be something very obvious since you are not going to be as familiar with your surroundings as you would be at home. Obvious landmarks, city government buildings, or public safety buildings (police stations, fire stations) are great choices for out of town family emergency meeting areas. You want these to be places that everyone knows about and can locate.

Each member of your family should be familiar with all of the possible meeting places. It is also worth noting that everyone should be aware of multiple routes to get to each of the places as well. Main roads could be closed by a marauding swarm of zombies or rendered impassible due to flood waters or trees brought down by high winds. Knowing multiple routes to safety could very well make the difference between being protected and being a statistic.

Family Emergency Communication Plans and Family Emergency Meeting Places should be reviewed at least once a year to make sure everyone has the most up-to-date information. You don't want to wait until a disaster happens to discover that you don't have someone's new cellphone number. Likewise, the aftermath of a tornado is not the most convenient time to remember that your Family Emergency Meeting Place was Uncle Bob's house and Uncle Bob moved out of the state when he retired last year.

There is an old adage that states "no good plan ever survives contact with the enemy" and that is very apt when trying to plan for responses to natural disasters. You will be trying to establish some type of order in an atmosphere of chaos. In order to ensure that your emergency plans have a reasonable chance of success, it is important that you practice them. Schedule a "test run" of your Family Emergency Plan at least once a year. Naturally you will want to let everyone know that you are planning a test just so they are not panicked, but by the same respect you might not want to let them know exactly when the test is happening. A good method for this is to contact everyone on your Family Emergency Communication Plan and let them know that you will be conducting a test of the plan next weekend at some time but don't tell them the exact day or time. This way they will know the messages you send are not in response to an actual disaster, but they will also be cognizant of the need to respond.

Once everyone is aware, then test the plan. Assume a disaster has struck and begin contacting people. Be creative in your ideas. Maybe the Zombie Apocalypse has happened. You and a few other people are safe in your house, but the roads into the neighborhood are all blocked by swarms of the living dead. Once everyone in your house is accounted for, begin contacting everyone not with you. Find out where they are and if they are safe where they are. If they are in a building, then you can assume they are safe. They answer you so they are alive and most likely barricaded in. If they are outside, maybe watching a kid's soccer game, then you should work with them to find a safe place for them to shelter.

Doing a few test runs of your Family Emergency Communication Plan will allow you to find the weak spots. Did everyone get your communication? Did they respond? Could they respond? Were you able to find safe places for everyone? Document what worked with your plan and what didn't work and then incorporate those changes so that the next time it goes more smoothly. The best time to find problems with your Family Emergency Plan is during one of these tests. Consequently, the worst time to find problems is when an actual disaster happens.

Organizing and Protecting Your Important Documents

We live in a digital age, but even so a great deal of your life is defined by several important pieces of paper. The loss of any of these pieces of paper could cause you some major problems. Anyone who has had their purse or wallet lost or stolen can attest to what a colossal pain in the neck it is to replace credit cards, debit cards, drivers licenses, and other forms of identification. Now let's imagine that you are forced to flee your house quickly in the middle of the night taking only the clothes on your back. Once you are safely outside, your entire house is destroyed along with all of the contents. This could be due to a tornado, a flash flood, or a house fire. Now you have the unfortunate task of trying to rebuild your life with absolutely nothing to start with. Any information you had regarding your insurance coverage, utility information, bank information, and even personal identification is all gone. Now you have the unenviable position of trying to rebuild your life from scratch with no documentation. This is not a position you ever want to be in.

In this section, I will discuss these important documents—both what they are and what you can do to collect them and keep them safe.

The documents you should be concerned about keeping safe are the documents that ultimately can provide proof about who you are and what you own. Some of them are obvious while others may be less so. Many of these documents are unique in that only one copy can exist at a time so (Zombie Apocalypse or disaster preparedness aside) it is still a really good idea to know where all of these are. For the sake of identification, I am referring to any type of document that can legally establish your identity—such as:

- Driver's license
- State issued ID card (a state Department of Motor Vehicles can issue an ID card which serves as legal identification without bestowing driving privileges on the cardholder)
- Passport
- Social Security card
- Birth certificate or Certificate of Naturalization
- Permanent Resident Card—aka "green card"
- Military service ID (United States Uniformed Services Privilege and Identification Card or Common Access Card)

While not being able to be used as a primary source of establishing your identity, the following documents can be used as secondary sources of establishing your identity and so are also very important:

- Marriage license
- Divorce decree
- Child custody paperwork
- Employer (or school) ID card
- Voter's registration card
- Automobile insurance card
- Health insurance card (this could be either Medicare or a private insurance company)

- Library card
- Amateur radio license
- Pilot's license
- Concealed firearm permit
- Deed for ownership of property
- Vehicle registration
- Vehicle title
- W-2 wage and tax statement

There are also many different documents that are equally important despite not being able to be used to establish your identity. Keeping these documents safe will benefit you in other ways. Those important documents would be:

- Utility bills—even if you don't keep a copy of each utility bill, you should have the account number and Customer Service telephone number for every utility.
- Insurance policies—home, renters, auto—whatever you have you should keep a copy of your most recent policy statement. Not only will this provide you with important things like your account number, your local agent's name, and the phone numbers needed to make a claim, but you will also know what is covered by your insurance policy and what is not covered.
- Investment records
- Income tax information—this is preferably a complete copy of your previous year's tax paperwork
- Pay stubs—just one should be sufficient although you should replace it every year due to withholding and benefit changes
- Employer benefit paperwork—if you get health, dental, and vision insurance through your employer, you should keep the paperwork for each benefit as they are likely through separate agencies
- Medicare/Medicaid paperwork
- VA Health benefit paperwork
- Will—this should also include any living wills
- Letter of Intent—Also known as a Letter of Instruction, this document is used to lay out your personal preferences for planning your estate. While not a legally binding document like a will, a Letter of Intent is generally used to specify whether you want to be buried or cremated, what type of memorial service (if any) you want, and the like. Morbid? Possibly, but a Letter of Intent acts as a "cheat sheet" for your executor (the person who is in charge of distributing your estate and seeing

to your final wishes). Think about it this way: this poor person has already had it hard enough. They had to watch you die, then be reanimated as a zombie and then get killed again. Don't you think they've already been through enough without having to wonder about if you wanted to be cremated or buried? Author's note: cremation is very effective against the Zombie Plague Virus.

- Financial and medical Powers of Attorney
- Contact information for your family doctor and dentist as well as any specialists or pediatricians your family uses
- A complete list of all medications and prescriptions you or anyone in your family takes along with the information on the prescribing doctor and pharmacy
- An up-to-date record of immunizations
- Information on any allergies, medical equipment or devices needed, disability documentation where applicable as well as any caregiver agency contact information
- Contact information for employers and/or supervisors, schools or colleges, your family's house of worship, social service providers, HomeOwners Associations, and a list of known and trusted home repair services

Now that you have you and your immediate family covered, what about your pets? Just like humans, the animals in our lives have documentation. Pet owners should also locate:

- Pet adoption information
- Registration information
- Vaccination records
- Any required tags (i.e., city dog tags, rabies vaccination tags, etc.)
- Microchip information if your pet is microchipped—this is also a good time to make sure the microchip contains your correct contact information
- A picture of you and your pet together as this can not only identify your pet, but can also help establish ownership

By now you probably have a rather substantial pile of documents. So, now what? You have all of this important documentation collected, now you need to keep it safe. The key to this? Redundancy. First and foremost, the original copies of these documents should never be the only copies you have. Now that you have all of your important documents collected into one place, you should immediately make a copy of them—or multiple copies of them. Obviously there are some things that a copy of is just that—a copy. For example, you cannot legally possess two driver's licenses or two passports. In cases like that, a copy might not prove useful for their original function (please don't drive a car while only carrying a copy of your driver's license); the copy can still be handy in helping you replace the original. A copy of your driver's license still has your driver's license number on it, for example. While you can't use that as legal proof that you are able to drive, the information from it can assist you at the DMV.

Once you have at least one copy of all of your important documents, then you need to determine how to keep them safe. Take one copy of everything and seal it in a large envelope. That packet should be stored somewhere outside of your house—maybe in a locked desk drawer at work or maybe with a trusted friend or relative. It's not so important where these copies are kept, just that they are as far away from your house as reasonably possible. This is to ensure that the documents will be safe should something catastrophic happen to your house. While you may implicitly trust your neighbors, it is still best to have at least one copy of your important documents outside of your immediate neighborhood. Wildfires, floods, tornadoes, and hurricanes can destroy whole neighborhoods so sometimes just across the street isn't far enough away to be secure.

Also, don't limit yourself to just one copy. If one backup is good, then two backups are better and three are even better. Remember: redundancy is the key to the safety of these documents. Keep one packet locked in a desk drawer at work. Send one to your friend who lives across town. Send another copy to a relative who lives in a different city or even a different state. Offer to store copies of their important documents for them in return. After all, you want them to be safe as well.

While you're going through all of the trouble of making copies of these documents, you might as well scan them so that you have electronic copies of them as well. Scanned documents obviously take up much less room than a stack of papers and they also allow you to have more versatility in your redundancy. Scan all of your important documents and save them to a USB drive that you can keep on your keychain, in a desk drawer at work, or send to a friend or relative for safe keeping.

Don't feel like you are limited to just storing the scanned documents on physical media, either. Online storage services like Dropbox (www.dropbox.com), Box (www.box.com), Google Drive (www.drive.google.com), Microsoft's OneDrive (www.onedrive.com), Backblaze (www.backblaze.com), Amazon Cloud Drive (www.amazon.com/

clouddrive), and Apple's iCloud (icloud.com) provide safe and secure online storage for your documents. Keep in mind that not all of these services are free, but many of them do offer tiered pricing plans depending on the amount of data you plan on storing. Aside from providing another layer of redundancy, online drive storage is very convenient since all you need to gain access to your important documents is an Internet connection.

Now that you have all of the copies of your important documents safe and secure in multiple places, it is time to consider what to do with the originals.

Naturally, you will not want to ship away your original documents. Those need to be kept secure and handy somewhere in or very near your house. A good way to do this is to store all of the original copies in some type of safe. The mention of a safe probably brings to mind imagery of a bank vault or a wall safe hidden behind a painting like you see in spy movies. While both of these are great options, they are not very practical for the average person. The type of safe I am referring to is a fireproof safe box or a document safe. A fireproof safe box is a metal container with thick walls that are filled with an insulating material (typically cement, gypsum, or vermiculite). It is very important to note that a fireproof safe box is actually fire **resistant** and not **fireproof**. Fireproof safe boxes are not designed to be fireproof (despite the name). The insulation in the walls of the box will keep the interior at a lower temperature for a period of time. Temperature extremes and how long that temperature will be maintained are variable based on the manufacture of the fireproof safe box.

Buying a Fireproof Safe Box

There are two major things to keep in mind when purchasing a fireproof safe box: the size of the box itself and the fireproof rating of the box.

The size of the box is self-explanatory. How much will it hold?. Fireproof safe boxes are sized based on the amount of available storage space inside them in cubic feet (length × width × height). Very small fireproof safe boxes are available with 0.15 cubic feet of available storage. This usually means a storage area of about 4.5" tall by 9.5" high by 6" deep. Obviously any papers stored in this would need to be folded. Larger fireproof safe boxes of around 0.28 cubic feet provide an interior storage area of sufficient size to store normal documents laid flat.

Fireproof safe boxes come in many different larger sizes with larger storage capacities. This also comes at a higher price. You should purchase a fireproof safe box based on the amount of paperwork you plan on storing in it—too small and you risk leaving something out, too big and you are paying for wasted space. Give yourself some room to grow as you don't want to have your fireproof safe box so tightly packed that you can't add another document or two should the need arise.

Fireproof safe boxes are given a fireproof rating. Most of them are tested and rated by Underwriters Laboratory (UL) and the inspection firm Intertek and given an "ETL" rating, which stands for Electrical Testing Laboratories, the certification division of Intertek responsible for certifying the testing. The testing and rating process is very rigorous. To receive a rating, a fireproof safe box is placed inside a furnace set to a specific temperature for a controlled amount of time. The fireproof safe box is then removed from the furnace, dropped from 30 stories, and then placed back into the furnace for another round of extreme temperatures.

Most fireproof safe boxes are rated to last 30 minutes at 1,550 °F (843 °C) at a minimum although many are now available with an ETL rating of one hour at 1,700 °F (927 °C). These ratings mean that the interior storage area of the box would be kept at a temperature lower than 350 °F (177 °C) even when the exterior of the box is subjected to these extremely hot temperatures. Given that normal paper will combust at a temperature of 451 °F (233 °C) (thanks to Ray Bradbury for that knowledge), this is sufficient protection for any paper stored inside.

Other types of media have different combustion temperatures. Digital media (CDs, DVDs, USB drives) will be ruined by temperatures over 125 °F (52 °C); tape and film will be destroyed by sustained temperatures around 150 °F (66 °C). This is important to keep in mind when you are deciding what items to store in your fireproof safe box.

It may seem counterintuitive that fireproof safe boxes are only rated to maintain a temperature for either 30 minutes or one hour since a house fire burns for a long time. While this is true, a fire in a room will generally reach its hottest point fairly quickly. A fire can only burn as long as there is fuel for it so while a burning room can reach temperatures approaching 2,000 °F (1,094 °C), these temperatures are typically located towards the ceiling of the room (since heat rises) and a room, once fully combusted, will burn itself out at a quite remarkable speed—another reason to flee a burning house as quickly as you can.

Some fireproof safe boxes are also waterproof. This is an added layer of protection in the case of a flood or for the simple fact that the fire department in fighting a house fire is going to dump a lot of water on it. A waterproof fireproof safe box is very handy to have since nothing would be more tragic than to have all of your documents survive a house fire only to be destroyed by the very same thing used to put the fire out.

Safe Deposit Box

Another perfectly valid option for storing your original copies of these important documents is a bank safe deposit box. Admittedly, this is more of an "old-school" option that many younger people have never encountered. For clarification, a safe deposit box (also called a safety deposit box) is a secure metal container used to store valuables. Safe deposit boxes are rented by banks for a small fee depending on the size of the box rented. The boxes are stored in the bank's vault and there are typically strict controls over who has access to the box. Aside from being stored in the vault, access to a safe deposit box is typically controlled by a pair of keys—you as the renter of the box will have one key and the bank will hold the other. The safe deposit box requires both keys to open the box. Some newer boxes are secured using biometric authentication (fingerprint or hand scanning). No matter the method used to secure the box, you can expect to have to show some form of identification and sign a form every time you access the safe deposit box.

Safe deposit boxes have been around since the 1800s and have been a popular way for people to protect their valuables. Due to the wide availability of fireproof safe boxes and their reasonable prices, safe deposit boxes at banks have lost popularity. You will most likely have to go to a larger branch of your bank to even find a safe deposit box—provided your bank still offers them for rent. They do still remain an attractive option for many people, though and they are definitely worth exploring.

Safe deposit boxes provide a great deal of safety and security, but there are some significant drawbacks to consider. First and foremost, access to the safe deposit box is strictly controlled. If the safe deposit box is secured by a key, you obviously need the key. The rental agreement on the safe deposit box also requires there to be a list of people who will have access to the safe deposit box. If your name is not on the list, you will not have access to the safe deposit box. If you do store your important documents in a safe deposit box, make sure you provide a list of the people who may need access to the box in your absence—your spouse, children, or other family members, for example.

Another thing to take into consideration is the fact that in order to have access to your safe deposit box, you must have access to the bank. A disaster can happen at any time whereas banks are only open during business hours and close on weekends and major holidays. Outside factors can prevent entry into the bank. Suppose the zombie horde has surrounded your local bank branch. Any bank personnel still inside probably have more on their mind than letting you in at the moment. In a more realistic scenario, during the Covid 19 global pandemic, many banks closed their lobbies to the public, leaving only drive-through and ATM access. Bank lobbies remained closed to the public for several weeks. If you had a safe deposit box that you needed access to during that time, you were effectively out of luck.

Insurance

The subject of insurance has been mentioned several times in this book so far and it does bear mentioning that if you are planning ways to make yourself as resilient as possible in the face of a natural disaster, insurance is very important.

If you are like many people, insurance is just another bill you pay and you may never think too much about it. This chapter of the book is about positioning yourself so that you can survive a natural disaster and return to normal life as you know it in the quickest amount of time and with the least amount of inconvenience. Having the correct insurance is a necessity to accomplish this.

There are many types of insurance, but the "big three" areas for coverage are for your person (health insurance/life insurance), what you drive (automotive insurance), and where you live (homeowner's or renter's insurance). For the purpose of this book, we will concentrate on the last type and discuss homeowner's or renter's insurance.

What is insurance after all?

At its core, insurance is a contract in which an individual receives financial protection or reimbursement against losses. In plain English, you make regular payments to your insurance company and their end of the bargain is that they will pay you back if your property gets damaged or destroyed. The contract is your insurance policy and you (of course) are the individual. Your insurance policy will clearly spell out how much your insurance company is obligated to pay you to make reparations for any losses to your property and under what circumstances those payouts will occur.

If you have never read your insurance policy, then please put this book down and go do so immediately—it is a contract, after all, and you should know what is in it. When reading your policy, there are some things to keep in mind. If you own a house, then you should have homeowner's insurance. Homeowner's insurance is written to cover your **dwelling** (your house), **other structures** (garages, decks, fences, sheds), and **personal property** (clothing, furniture, appliances, any "stuff" in your house). There should be a section detailing **loss of use** (compensation if you need to relocate from your house due to covered damage to the structure), **personal liability** (coverage if you are sued due to an accidental injury to another person while on your property), and **medical protection** (payments to cover the medical bills for a person who is injured in an accident on your property).

Manufactured homes, condominiums, and farms all have slightly more specialized types of homeowner's insurance. Policies for condominiums, for example, are written with a provision to cover only the portion of the condominium that it is your responsibility to maintain and repair. Renter's insurance is obviously for people who rent rather than own a house. Renter's insurance naturally will provide no coverage for the dwelling since the building is owned by another party. Renter's insurance will provide you coverage for **personal property** (clothing, furniture), **loss of use** (compensation if you need to relocate due to damaged to the building that you are renting), **personal liability** (coverage if you are sued due to an accidental injury to another person while on your property), **medical payments** (payments to cover the medical bills for a person who is injured in an accident in your property), and **property damage to others** (coverage in case you accidentally break someone else's property).

Your insurance policy will detail the specific types of losses (or "perils" in insurance-speak) that you are covered for. These typically include:

- Fire
- Malfunctioning plumbing
- Damage caused by malfunctioning heating, air conditioning, and sprinkler systems
- Falling objects
- Civil unrest
- Explosions
- Hail
- Wildfire
- Hurricanes
- Theft
- Tornadoes
- Vehicular damage
- Volcanoes

You will notice that the particular types of perils are very specifically laid out—fire damage being classified differently than wildfire damage, for example. If a particular peril is not specifically spelled out as being covered, then you should assume that it is not covered. One example of this is the fact that damage from a hurricane is different (from the insurance company's point of view) from damage from the storm surge that usually accompanies a hurricane. Storm surge damage is considered to be flood damage. Typically insurance policies **do not** cover flood damage or earthquake damage. Both of these require separate policies.

The best time to ensure that you have the proper (and proper amount) of insurance coverage is before a catastrophe strikes. Read your insurance policy thoroughly and understand it. If there is something you don't understand or you think something is lacking, call your insurance agent immediately and make an appointment to get it resolved. Not having the proper insurance coverage can be financially devastating.

I know of a person who learned this lesson the hard way. He and his wife were hosting a Christmas party and had a houseful of guests when the unthinkable happened—raw sewage began surging up through all of the drains and toilets in his basement. Obviously, his Christmas party ended early and with a great deal of embarrassment, but his tribulations were not over. He called a plumber to find out what had happened. It turned out that tree roots had grown into and through the sewage lines between his house and the street.

He called his insurance company and was delivered the terrible news that he was not covered for this. His policy would have covered this event had it been caused by faulty plumbing in his house. It would have also covered this event had it been caused by a problem with the city's sewer lines. Since the problem was caused by damage to the sewer lines outside of his house and technically on his property, that event was not covered. His entire yard had to be excavated and new sewer lines run and the cost of this had to come out of his pocket. This was naturally very expensive.

Having heard this news, I called my insurance agent and presented the same scenario to him only to discover that I would not have been covered either. I quickly added a supplemental policy and learned a valuable lesson—read and understand your insurance policy. Know what you are covered for and what you are not covered for. Failure to do so could be very costly.

Now you have found a way to protect all of your important documents, establish communication with your family to keep them safe, and have made sure that catastrophic damage to your residence would not prove to be financially devastating to you. Are there other things you can do to be prepared? Of course there are!

First Aid

When the shambling horde of the restless undead make their way into your town, it is safe to say that your doctor's appointment that day has been well and truly canceled. In a more practical sense, you could slip and fall and injure yourself while trying to dig out from a blizzard and the roads could be treacherous. In the event of a large-scale disaster, emergency services could very well be overwhelmed or possibly unable to get to your location. The ability to perform basic first aid is an invaluable skill and could potentially save a life.

Granted, if you are not a first responder or a trained medical professional, you will not be qualified to perform advanced techniques, but there are basic first aid skills that everyone should know.

First and foremost are the Three Ps of first aid: **Preserve Life**, **Prevent Further Injury**, and **Promote Recovery**. At its core, a knowledge of basic first aid skills will give you the training to do what you can to save an injured person's life, to do what you can to keep them from sustaining further injuries, and to do what you can to help them heal. You may not be a trained medical professional, but you may also be the only other person on the scene to help. Accidents can happen quickly and even in the largest cities, emergency services can still take several minutes to arrive. Applying the Three Ps could very well mean the difference between life and death.

First aid classes are offered by the National Safety Council (NSC) and the American Red Cross. The skills taught in those classes can give you the knowledge to control bleeding, care for wounds and injuries, as well as treat poisoning or choking situations, sprains, heat exhaustion, hypothermia, burns, and bone fractures. First aid training also covers administering CPR and the usage of an Automated External Defibrillator (AED).

First aid techniques are different for adults, children and infants and the course will prepare you for all scenarios. For those of us with pets, the American Red Cross also offers a basic pet first aid course which covers understanding a pet's vital signs, treating breathing and cardiac emergencies, wounds, bleeding, seizures, and basic preventative care for cats and dogs. As easily as you could be cut off from visiting a doctor, you could also be cut off from being able to visit a veterinarian.

Locate Your Utility Cut-Offs

Whether you own or rent your home, you should be aware of the locations of the main shut-off locations for all of your major utilities. This would include the location of the main power breaker and the main shut-off valves for water and gas. At the sign of any widespread system failure such as a short circuit, electrical fire, major plumbing leak, or gas leak—the ability to quickly turn off a utility at its source could protect your house from sustaining extensive damage.

Navigate Using a Map

GPS units and cell phones with driving directions have made it easier than ever before to navigate. Even the most basic navigation app can now accept voice input and reroute you in real time to avoid traffic or speed traps or even just tell you the shortest route to your favorite coffee shop. This technology is great and I personally rely on it heavily, but it does have its limitations. Once the dead rise from the grave to feast upon the living, we can't expect our technology to work as seamlessly as it does now. Even barring the Zombie Apocalypse, cellphones can be damaged. Screens can be cracked. They can get wet. Water and electronics are never a good mix. Cell phones also run on batteries and batteries naturally have a limited run time. There are still areas of the country where cell reception is poor and this can be exacerbated by possible damage to cell towers due to high winds, storms, or other natural disasters.

Heavy cloud cover can also inhibit GPS signals, leaving you stranded if you rely on a GPS to get around. It is also not unheard of for GPS directions to be inaccurate or incorrect. It might take some time for the maps in your GPS to get updated so new roads, bridges, or routes might not appear for a while. It is not unheard of for a GPS to navigate you through a route which may technically be shorter, but not necessarily safer. In 2009, a woman and her son were driving through Death Valley National Park and navigating by their GPS. The GPS directed them down a little used dirt road which (unbeknownst to them) was not well maintained. Their vehicle became stuck and they then became lost. Park rangers found them a week later, but unfortunately the child had died by that time. As awful as this sounds, it happens so frequently that rescue workers have coined the term "death by GPS" to describe incidents like this. All things being equal, the ability to read a good old-fashioned paper map and navigate your way around without using technology is a very important skill and very well could save your life.

To navigate your way through an area using a map, you need a paper map of the area (obviously) and a compass. During the day under a clear sky it is easy to get your bearings using the sun as a guide, but a compass is necessary for when it is cloudy, dark, or you can't clearly see the sky because of thick smoke or being under the cover of a thick canopy of trees.

There are several great resources to learn the skill of navigating by map. There are books, videos, and websites dedicated to the subject. If you are the type of person who would like more "real world" experience, you should look into the sport of Orienteering.

Originally designed as a training exercise in land navigation for the military, Orienteering has developed into a sport participated in by tens of thousands of people from all around the world. There are even Orienteering events in the World Games. At its core, Orienteering is an event in which a participant uses a map and compass to navigate through a specific area and visit certain waypoints. Competitive Orienteering events are timed and the winners navigate to all of the waypoints in the shortest amount of time. Many of the events are not competitive and provide excellent family-friendly ways to spend time outdoors and to improve your skill at navigating using just a map and compass. There are Orienteering events for walkers and runners known as Foot Orienteering. There are also Mountain Bike Orienteering, Ski Orienteering, and Trail Orienteering events. Amateur radio operators also conduct Amateur Radio Direction Finding or Radio Orienteering events in which participants must navigate through an area using a map and compass to locate particular radio transmitters.

Final Thoughts

Whether you're planning on the Zombie Apocalypse or a natural disaster, this chapter was designed to help you lay the groundwork for making sure you are as ready as possible when the unexpected occurs. Fires, floods, tornados, hurricanes, earthquakes, storms, power outages, alien invasions, giant monster attacks, or the outbreak of the Zombie Apocalypse can happen any time and without warning. In the event of a disaster like one of these happening, there is a very real chance that you could be left to your own devices and (more importantly) expected to be self-sufficient for an extended period of time. This could be as little as a few days or potentially as long as several weeks. You may not have access to emergency services or even basic communication during that time and things may seem pretty grim.

If you have seen as many horror movies as I have (and I assume you have by the nature of your reading this book), then you know that eventually the zombies die off, the aliens leave, the giant monster goes back into the ocean, and life does get back to normal. The information in the chapter is designed to allow you to get back to a normal life as quickly and easily as possible once the disaster has passed. The remainder of this book will discuss survivability and self-sufficiency in more detailed aspects for particular scenarios. One last piece of knowledge should be at the core of your "forewarned is forearmed" thought process. That is the Survivability Rule of 3.

The Survivability Rule of 3 means that a person can generally survive:

- 3 minutes without breathable air
- 3 hours in harsh weather without shelter
- 3 days without water
- 3 weeks without food

These are the core building blocks when planning for how to actually survive a natural disaster. Breathable air, shelter, drinkable water, and food are the absolute minimum you need to survive. Locating (and keeping) them should be your ultimate goal and the foundation on which you build any survival plan. That being said, you are now armed with the knowledge of how to prepare yourself before a disaster strikes. Subsequent chapters will discuss dealing with various disaster scenarios as they occur.

Chapter 2

The *Night of the Living Dead* Scenario

Night of the Living Dead was an independent horror film released in 1968. It was written and directed by George Romero and it has become the seminal zombie movie. If you have read this far in this book (or if you have managed to make it this far in life) and you have somehow never seen this film, stop what you are doing. Put this book down, and go watch it.

The film opens with brother and sister Johnny and Barbara driving along a rural road. They make their way to a cemetery—specifically the Evans City Cemetery outside of Evans City, Pennsylvania, a small town located north of Pittsburgh, Pennsylvania. They are making the journey with the intent of placing a memorial wreath on their father's grave. The drive has taken a while and it is early in the evening when they arrive—Barbara even mentions the fact that it is eight o'clock and still daylight. This is beneficial since in most areas of the country, it is illegal to be in a cemetery after dark. It would definitely have been a waste of the three hour drive if they had arrived too late. They arrive at the cemetery and Barbara begins looking around for their father's grave.

Johnny notices that the car radio, which had gone silent a while back, suddenly starts broadcasting again. Johnny assumes the radio station had technical difficulties and turns the radio off without listening to the beginning of the frantic sounding transmission. He exits the car to join Barbara in the cemetery. They locate their father's grave and place the wreath on it. Barbara spends a few minutes in silent prayer over the grave while being chided by Johnny. She admits that being at the cemetery unnerves her and Johnny, being a typical brother, proceeds to antagonize her about it, setting the stage for his famous line "They're coming to get you, Barbara." Seeing someone else in the cemetery, Johnny continues his ribbing, "Look! There's one now!"

Barbara becomes angry at Johnny's taunts—doubly so now that someone else has noticed the way he was acting. It was probably very embarrassing for her to have another mourner see her brother acting in such a disrespectful manner. Any embarrassment she was feeling quickly fades away when the man moves closer to them and lunges to attack Barbara. Johnny and the man fight and Johnny is thrown to the ground, striking his head on a tombstone. With her brother lying motionless and presumably dead and the man still trying to attack her, Barbara runs to the car only to find that Johnny had the keys with him.

She locks herself in the car (this is 1968 after all—before the time of power door locks), but the man has followed her. He pounds wildly on the windows before picking up a large rock and shattering the passenger one. His hands grope inside for Barbara and she struggles to get away. She releases the parking brake. The car, being parked at the top of a hill, begins to roll downward. Near the bottom, the car veers off the road and strikes a tree. The man is still in pursuit so Barbara flees the car to look for a safe place. She runs to a house and finds the door conveniently open. She rushes inside and closes and locks the door behind her.

Not immediately finding the owners, she arms herself with a kitchen knife and searches the house until she finds the telephone. She tries the phone, but unfortunately the line is dead. Searching the rest of the house, Barbara finds the half-eaten corpse of the house's owner. That discovery coupled with the fact that there are more zombies (fun fact: the word "zombie" is never used to refer to the creatures in the movie. Instead, the terms "those things," "ghouls," and "flesh eaters" are used) surrounding the house, Barbara panics and tries to flee. As she leaves the house, she runs into Ben, another survivor looking for shelter.

Ben sees that the shock of the situation is getting to Barbara so he rushes them both back inside the house and begins to secure the house by boarding up the windows and doors. The noise of the fortification effort alerts others who have taken shelter in the cellar—Tom and Judy, a teenage couple who came to the house for shelter after hearing emergency broadcasts on the radio telling of brutal murders that were happening—and the Cooper family, Harry, Helen, and their daughter Karen. The Coopers took shelter in the house after a group of zombies overran their car and attacked them. In the ensuing struggle, the zombies attacked and bit Karen and she has subsequently fallen very ill.

As the survivors assess their situation, they discover that the house has a radio and a television and those are still operational and receiving broadcasts. Both the radio and television are receiving similar grim transmissions—the entire Eastern coast of the United States is being plagued by an unexplained wave of mass murders. Bodies of the dead are reanimating, attacking, and killing the living. They establish the trope that zombies can be killed by sufficient damage to the brain—either a blow to the head or a bullet. The broadcasts also mention a theory that the reanimation of the bodies is a result of radiation from a space probe returning from Venus that exploded in Earth's atmosphere. The broadcasts also list several emergency shelters that have been set up in local hospitals, high schools, fire stations, and community centers.

The survivors get into a rather spirited discussion as to whether they would be safer in the house or in the cellar. This debate ends with Harry and Helen opting to stay in the cellar with their daughter while the remainder of the survivors stay upstairs. The survivors come up with a plan to drive to one of the emergency shelters while trying to find some medical attention for Karen on the way. Tom and Judy leave the house in an attempt to fight their way past the zombies to reach Tom's truck, but an accident costs them their lives and destroys the truck in the process. Now trapped in the house with no escape, the remaining survivors make a last stand as the zombies break through the barricades they erected. In the ensuing chaos, Barbara is attacked and carried away by the zombies (ironically, by the reanimated zombie of her brother Johnny), Harry is killed, Karen dies from her injuries and then reanimates and kills her mother.

Ben, now the only survivor, retreats to the cellar and barricades himself inside. He waits in the cellar all night until he no longer hears the zombies' footsteps. Once the sounds from upstairs stop, Ben cautiously makes his way out of the cellar to investigate. He finds the horde of zombies gone and the house empty and quiet. He peers out through one of the broken windows to see how the situation looks in the outside world. Unbeknownst to him, there is a group of armed men roaming the area killing off the remaining zombies. One of the men sees Ben's face in the window and, mistaking him for a zombie, shoots him dead. The movie ends with still shots of the men gathering the corpses and burning them in large piles.

As you can imagine, movies featuring the Zombie Apocalypse are rarely ever uplifting "feel-good" films. From the aspect of surviving a natural disaster, however, the survivors made some smart choices along the way. After the zombie attacked her in the graveyard, Barbara found herself in a situation that is not at all uncommon for someone in the wake of a disaster. She suddenly found herself outside and alone in a situation that was beyond her control and that she knew very little about. All she did know was that she was not safe where she was, so she made the intelligent decision to leave that area quickly and find some type of shelter. Once inside the house with the other survivors, they set about boarding up the doors and windows in order to secure the house. They had found shelter from the zombies and worked to make their shelter even more secure against an outside threat.

Once they had secured themselves in the house, they attempted to establish some form of communication with the outside world, but the phone did not work. Their next option was the radio and television—both of which were providing news on the ongoing disaster and information on shelters that people could go to for protection. It is not unreasonable to think that the survivors could have just stayed hunkered down in the house until the zombies outside had been dealt with. Their choice to leave the house and go to one of the emergency shelters was not a bad choice, either. In a perfect world, they should have waited until it was daylight before trying to leave, but the perceived medical situation with Karen added a level of urgency to their decision.

Another notable point is the fact that all of the events in the movie take place in less than 24 hours. Barbara and Johnny arrive at the graveyard at about 8:00 p.m. The survivors barricade themselves in the house and fight off the zombies for most of that night and the movie ends with the arrival of the armed posse the next morning when you are led to believe that life is beginning to return to normal. Granted, later movies in this series show that the Zombie Apocalypse was not limited to just the East Coast and eventually affected the entire planet, but for the purpose of this chapter we are going to operate within the parameters of the film to establish a timeframe that the natural disaster of the zombie threat was contained within 24 to possibly 72 hours.

This is an important point in disaster preparedness because 95 percent of the interruptions to normal life (power outages, service interruptions, road closures, etc.) are resolved within the first 72 hours after a disaster strikes. This also establishes a great starting point for disaster preparedness—meaning at the bare minimum you should be prepared for the need to be completely self-sufficient for 72 hours. Obviously all natural disasters are different and will affect both your environment and the infrastructure that serves it in different ways. If high winds knock down a tree onto some power lines, you will be without electricity until the damage gets repaired but your cell phone would still work and the municipal water running to your house would continue to provide you with clean drinking water.

Suppose a flood or snowstorm makes travel outside of your neighborhood treacherous or impossible. You may still have power, water, and heat, but what about sufficient food supplies? That is the purpose of this chapter—to guide you in preparation to be fully self-sufficient for up to 72 hours so you can safely and relatively comfortably ride out the interruption of some (or all) utilities due to a tornado, high wind event, blizzard, flood, or small scale zombie outbreak.

So now the disaster has struck. Be it tornado, fire, flash flood, wind storm, power outage, or an over-curious neighbor has read passages from the Necronomicon causing the dead to come back to life—the event has happened and now you must expect to be self-sufficient to some degree for the next 24 to 72 hours. What does that look like? Remember the Survivability Rule of 3 (see end of previous chapter): 3 minutes, 3 hours, 3 days, 3 weeks.

While these are all necessary things to remember, the first and foremost thing to consider is your immediate safety.

Ensure Your Own Personal Safety

As soon as Barbara was attacked by the zombie in the cemetery, she made the obvious choice to get as far away from the danger as possible. This is essential to any decisions you make during the course of a disaster. Your personal safety is your number one priority. There is a reason that the preflight instructions on airplanes tell you to affix your oxygen mask first before tending to those of your children. While it may sound selfish, the harsh reality is that you cannot be of any help to anyone else if you are killed or badly injured. Regardless of the situation, your first goal is to ensure your own safety. Get out of the burning house. Move to higher ground away from the rising water. Take shelter during a tornado. Run away from the zombies that are trying to eat you. They move slowly, remember, so unless you get yourself surrounded by a large group of them, you are probably going to be able to make a break for it and outdistance them.

Breathable Air

At this point we begin to look at the Survivability Rule of 3. First and most important on that list is breathable air. It doesn't take a survival expert to realize why this is the first item on the list. If you cannot breathe, then no other survival preparations really matter.

There are many things that can contribute to making the air dangerous to breathe. Dust and smoke contain particles that can be harmful if inhaled. A fire will produce harmful smoke, but it will also produce heat and fumes from the burning material. Superheated air is very dangerous to breathe as it can burn the inside of your lungs. Fumes from burning material can be difficult to breathe or even toxic, depending on what type of material is burning. Even basic household chemicals and building materials will generate dangerous fumes when combusted. Non-burning structures can have risks as well. Old buildings were insulated with asbestos and, even though asbestos is no longer used, it can still be present in dangerous levels in old structures. Areas that have been damp for a long period of time may have developed mold growths. Exposure to common black mold (*Stachybotrys chartarum*) can cause problems for people with chronic respiratory conditions and flu-like symptoms for people without preexisting respiratory conditions.

In short, there are many things that can be in the air that can make it harmful for you to breathe. Like any other source of harm, you should try to get away from the source of the polluted air if you can. If you are in the area of a chemical spill, for example, you should just get far away. While there are items of protective gear that will allow you to safely navigate through a hazardous waste spill, this is the type of gear that typically only trained professionals have access to. Your safest course of action is to ensure your own personal safety and get far away from the area.

When it comes to protecting your airway, the basic principle is that you want to create a barrier between you and the environment. In other words, you want to have your mouth and nose covered by something that will help prevent anything harmful from getting into your mouth, nose, and lungs. There are many ways to accomplish this and I will discuss them in order of effectiveness from least effective to most effective.

1. **No protection**—Obviously not wearing any type of protection is the least effective. Covering your mouth and nose with your hand or trying to hold your breath will not provide you with any real means of protection. Anything you can do is better than this method.
2. **Makeshift face covering**—Wrapping a bandana or piece of cloth around your mouth and nose will give you a certain amount of protection. Make sure the cloth covers both your nose and mouth and that the cloth fits tightly against your face since any gaps will defeat the purpose by letting unfiltered air in. Moisten the cloth with some water to help trap any particulate matter in the air (dust, smoke, etc.)—just keep in mind that you want it **lightly** moistened.
3. **Disposable face covering**—Once just the realm of

woodworkers and people with allergies, disposable face coverings have become commonplace to everyone after the Covid-19 pandemic. Disposable face coverings are available for purchase in bulk at most hardware stores, but by now you've probably got several tucked away somewhere. Since they are purpose-built to provide respiratory protection, they provide better protection than makeshift face coverings. They come in many shapes and sizes, but do they all provide equal protection? In short: no. First and foremost, it is important to understand the difference between a dust mask (or "nuisance" mask) and a respirator mask.

Dust masks are made of paper. They are very lightweight and flimsy and most notably only have one strap. They do not form a tight seal against your face and so they provide you very little protection against inhaling particulate matter from the air. If you have any of these that you are using as protective equipment, do yourself a favor and just get rid of them and purchase some respirator masks instead.

Respirator masks have two straps which allows them to sit tightly against your face when properly fitted. The entire mask is made of a filtering material. Some of them have vents while others do not. The vents act as a one-way valve opening when you breathe out and closing when you breathe in. This is designed to make these types of masks easier to breathe in since the air you exhale flows out of the mask more freely. The important thing to note is that all respirator masks have a Letter Class rating and a number rating, which designate the conditions under which the respirator mask was designed to be used. There are three Letter Classes—N, R, and P. A Class N respirator mask simply means the mask is made of a material that is not oil resistant. A Class R respirator mask is oil resistant, and a Class P respirator mask is oil proof.

The number rating classifies the percentage of particles that are at least 0.3 microns in diameter that the respirator mask will filter out. The most common rating is 95 which means the respirator mask will filter out 95 percent of particles in the air that are at least 0.3 microns in size. Respirator masks are also available in 99 and 100 which will filter out 99 percent and 99.7 percent of particles respectively. This means that the common N95 respirator mask is a mask that is made of a material that is not oil resistant and is designed to filter out 95 percent of the particles in the air that are at least 0.3 microns in size. As a point of reference, a particle of Anthrax is about 1 micron in size, Asbestos is 0.7 microns, mold spores are 10 microns, sawdust is 30 microns, and smoke from burning synthetic materials is about 1 micron.

While it may seem the best practice to always wear N100 respirator masks since they technically provide more protection, it is worth noting that a respirator mask rated at 99 or 100 can be more difficult to comfortably breathe through. The higher filtration rate of a mask rated at 99 or 100 essentially means the holes that allow the outside air to filter through are smaller and so more force is required to move the air in and out.

4. **Cartridge-based respirator masks**—These are respirator masks that rely on replaceable filtration cartridges to clean the air instead of the filtration happening as air is drawn through the material of the mask itself. These masks are larger and generally more expensive, but they provide the best protection against particulate matter. Since the masks are larger, they are designed to have a better fit. They are more easily adjustable to give you a good seal against your face. Some of them cover just your mouth and nose while others will cover your entire face. This serves to provide you with added protection for your eyes. Since the protection is provided by the replaceable cartridges instead of the mask itself, these types of respirator masks can provide a higher grade of protection than even an N100 mask. Some of these respirator masks can use cartridges rated as CBRN which stands for *Chemical, Biological, Radiological,* and *Nuclear* so these masks will protect you from everything from smoke and dust to chemical weapons, biological weapons, and even radioactive fallout.

The tradeoff for this type of protection is cost. Respirator masks like this start at about $100 and can easily cost $200 or more. CBRN cartridges are also about $100 each and must be replaced after they lose their effectiveness. These types of masks look very similar to the military style gas mask. For a more relevant analogy, during the early stages of a zombie virus outbreak you often see military and medical personnel wearing these types of masks in quarantine or decontamination areas.

The most important practice in wearing any type of face covering is wearing it properly—meaning your mouth and nose are both covered and the mask fits tightly against your face with no gaps for air to get in. The next most important idea is to understand that even the best mask has a limited lifespan of effectiveness. The time that a mask remains effective depends on several factors, but the type of mask and the type of environment are the biggest factors. The easiest way to know if your mask has reached the end of its useful life is to examine it. If you are wearing a mask in a smoky or dusty environment and you notice that your mask has become dirty or discolored, then it is probably time to change into a fresh one. Some masks may not be so easy to judge—the cartridges in cartridge-based respirator masks, for example. In these cases, follow the manufacturer's recommendations for the estimated lifespan of the mask or cartridge based on the hazards in the environment you are using it in.

Sealing Off a Room

There have been canonical references to the idea that the zombie virus is an airborne virus. In the television show "The Walking Dead," the origins of the zombie virus are never explained but the survivors do come to an understanding that all living humans have become contaminated by contact with something (either airborne, food borne, or water borne) that doesn't affect them while they are living but causes them to reanimate as a zombie after they die regardless of whether they were bitten by a zombie or not. In the *Return of the Living Dead* film series, we are introduced to the chemical 2-4-5 Trioxin, the gas of which can turn living people into a particular kind of zombie known as a Triombie. The chemical 2-4-5 Trioxin will also reanimate corpses into zombies as well. In *Return of the Living Dead*, the 2-4-5 Trioxin gas is released into the atmosphere by the cremation of a Triombie. Once in the atmosphere, the gas mixes with water droplets in the clouds and falls back onto a cemetery as contaminated rain. The Trioxin rain then seeps into the ground where it makes contact with the bodies buried there and they all reanimate as zombies to wreak havoc across the community.

The best way to protect yourself against the potential release of an airborne zombie virus agent (or other dangerous airborne chemicals) is to know how (and when) to properly seal off a room of your house. Doing so will give you the ability to isolate yourself and your family in an area that is separated from the air outside and any toxins it may contain. The idea behind this is to be able to provide a safe place for you and your family where you can shelter yourselves in clean, breathable air until the air outside of your house is safe to breathe once again. Note that this is not a long-term solution. Generally speaking you would expect to stay in your sealed room for a few hours at most.

Seeing as how this is something you are going to want to do very rapidly, it is a good idea to pick the room ahead of time so that you can make some initial preparations. An ideal room for this would be an interior room with few (if any windows). It would also be better if the room was on the smaller side, but not so small that you can't be comfortable in it. You could be sheltered in this area for several hours so a closet or a small bathroom would not be the most comfortable choice. A room above ground level is a better choice than a room on the first floor or underground if that is an option. Many chemical agents are heavier than air and so the gasses will stay close to the ground. Being higher than ground level will provide you with more protection.

When a situation arises that would necessitate you using your sealed room, you will be advised by local authorities. At that point you should:

- Make your way into the room as quickly as possible.
- Bring your family and any pets with you into the room.
- Bring your emergency supply kit so that you will have access to all of your supplies and will not need to leave the room for anything once you are inside.
- Once you and your family are all safely in the room, close (and lock) all doors and windows.
- Turn off any fans, air conditioners, forced air heating units, or any other device that moves air into the room.
- Seal all of the windows, doors, and air vents. Windows should be sealed by covering them with plastic sheets. The sheets should be at least 2" larger than the windows to ensure a complete seal. Tape the corners of the plastic sheets up first using duct tape, then tape down the edges of the plastic sheets. Be sure to tape over the **entire edge** leaving no gaps.
- Seal off any air vents in the room using a similar method. If the vents cannot be sealed by covering them with plastic (if they are on a carpeted floor, for example), then remove the vent cover and stuff the vent itself with towels, clothes, or rags to block it off.
- Seal off all doors in the room by covering the edges of the door frame with duct tape and stuffing towels, clothes, or rags under the door.
- Cover any electrical outlets with plastic and duct tape the same way you would cover a window. Pay special attention to outlets on exterior walls. No house is airtight and air will find its way in through the smallest gap. Outlets on exterior walls can allow drafts into your house. Don't believe me? Hold your hand up to an electrical outlet on a cold, windy winter day and see if you don't feel cool air coming in around it.
- Once you are safely sealed in the room, activate your Family Emergency Communication Plan—contact any friends and

family that are not in the room with you to let them know you are safe and to establish their location and safety.

- Stay informed by listening to the radio, a news app on your phone, or the Internet. Once the danger has passed, the authorities will let you know when it is safe to exit your room and how to maintain your safety once outside.

While you are sheltering in your sealed room, you should make an effort to keep some distance between you and any windows and doors. No amount of plastic and duct tape is going to make a completely airtight seal. The seal will be good enough that the room might begin to get stuffy and uncomfortable—especially if there are several people in it. Keep in mind that this is only a temporary measure until the outside air is safe to breathe again. Try to keep everyone in the room (yourself included) as quiet and calm as possible. The situation is going to be stressful enough without panic and uncontrolled emotions adding to it. You will need to be mentally prepared for the fact that your wits, your training, and your preparedness (hopefully learned from this book) is what is going to allow you to make it through.

Choose your designated safe room ahead of time. This allows you to communicate this to everyone in your family so they will immediately know where to go in the event of an emergency. This also allows you to prepare the room ahead of time. Using your safe room to store some of your supplies accomplishes two goals—not only will you have a secure and well-known storage space, but you won't have to worry about trying to get those supplies into the room when you need to use it. You can also save valuable time by pre-cutting plastic sheets to the correct size for the window, doors, vents, and outlets in the room. Cut them to the appropriate size, mark them with permanent marker as to their location, and store them in the room with your other supplies. This will allow you to quickly and easily seal the room in an emergency.

Shelter

After your own safety and access to clean air, the next step is ensuring you have some type of shelter from the elements. For the purpose of this chapter, this is most likely going to be your house or possibly your workplace. One of the principal concepts behind a secure shelter is the idea of keeping what is outside from getting in. In *Night of the Living Dead*, this was accomplished by Ben and Barbara boarding up the doors and windows of the house that the survivors were sheltering in. While you probably won't need to worry about barricading out the living dead, it is not out of line to think that you might need to secure some doors or windows. Tornadoes, strong winds, hail, and other types of storms can send debris through windows or damage your roof. If you are planning on sheltering in place in your house, any type of damage like that will need to be addressed quickly.

As soon as it is safe for you to do so, you should walk around your shelter (both inside and out) looking for any damage. Inside you should look for damage to windows or doors as well as any signs of water coming in. A leak in the ceiling of a room, for example, is a sure sign of damage to the roof. The outside of the structure should also be thoroughly examined. Check your roof for damage while checking the outside of your windows and doors. Remove any tree branches or debris from your house. If you have any pieces of siding or guttering partially hanging from your house, go ahead and remove them so any further wind will not cause more damage. Missing siding and damaged gutters are generally more cosmetic and will not cause major problems if not immediately repaired. You will want to have those things fixed at some point, but since your immediate survival doesn't depend on them, you can leave them for another day.

You should definitely be on the lookout for serious problems and address them as quickly as you can. If your roof is damaged, you can nail a tarp over the damaged area to at least keep the rain out of your house. Broken windows can be problematic as well. Clear away the broken glass (while wearing gloves) and patch the hole by covering it with something. Smaller breaks can be covered with a plastic sheet or piece of cardboard duct taped over the hole. Larger windows or more extensive damage may require you to cover the gap with a tarp or to even board up the window entirely. If you examine the exterior of your house and find large cracks in the walls or the foundation, then you should start looking at another place to take shelter as the structure of your house may have become unstable and dangerous to be in.

Your shelter is safe when everything that is on the outside will stay on the outside. This can mean anything from rain, wind, and snow to hordes of the walking dead.

Water

The next item on the Survivability Rule of 3 is access to clean, drinkable water. The average person needs 1 gallon of water per day for drinking and sanitation purposes. Since the focus of this chapter is an event lasting no more than 72 hours, this means you will need 3 gallons of water available for yourself and each person you plan on sheltering with you. While the first thing that comes to mind is to start stockpiling water, that is probably not necessary for the average person. Take some time and conduct an inventory of what you have accessible to you currently. Most people have plenty of beverages already in their refrigerator. It's also not unusual for people to have some bottled water in a pantry or closet. It is very likely that your situation won't be dire enough that you will run out of drinkable water in a matter of a few days.

It is also worth remembering that you will very likely still have access to your municipal water supply unless the disaster causes a disruption in the water lines or other infrastructure. Municipal water systems will still continue to function even with no power—at least for a period of time. Municipal water systems are gravity fed with the water pressure being provided by pumping stations. The next time you are out in your community, locate your community's water tower. You will find that it is going to be located at or near the highest geographical point in the community. Clean, treated water is pumped into a community's water tower. The water tower is designed to hold enough water to serve the community's water needs for a day. A fresh supply of clean water is pumped back in to fill the tank when water (and power) use is at its lowest—typically in the wee hours of the morning.

Water pressure is provided by a combination of the pressure of gravity from the water tower being located at the highest point in the community and supplemented by water pumping stations. Obviously in a blackout the pumping stations are not going to be running, but that generally doesn't stop the water in your taps from still running although even gravity fed municipal water systems will eventually stop if the power is out long enough. Generally speaking, this is roughly 24 hours. If you are experiencing a power outage that you have reason to believe will be lengthy, build up a water reserve by filling pots, pans, and even the bathtub. Fill up any container that can be used to hold water. In the film *28 Days Later*, Frank and his daughter Hannah collect rain water by placing pots and pans on the roof of their building. In a pinch, anything that can hold water will be helpful.

At one point the conventional wisdom said that you could drink the water from the toilet tank in an emergency. I would not recommend that—especially if you have ever used any type of cleaning chemical in the tank. Those cleaners contain bleach and other harsh chemicals that make the water in the toilet tank unsafe to drink. One look at the bright blue color of the water some of these cleaners leave behind should be enough to make you think twice about drinking it! It is also worth noting that since water is gravity fed, taps on the upper floors of a house will stop producing water before taps on lower floors so if you are looking to fill containers, start on your upper floors and finish on your lower floors (or basement).

On a similar note regarding water and sanitation, many people are unaware that your standard household toilet will continue to work even if you have no power or running water. The question of power should be fairly obvious as your toilet is not plugged into an electrical outlet, but ask anyone in emergency services how many times they are asked this question.

When you press down the lever on a toilet, a flapper in the tank opens and allows the water in the tank to go rushing into the toilet bowl. The bowl fills to the point that water begins to flow into a part of the toilet you never see called a *trapway*. Water rushing over the top of the trapway causes suction to draw the water from the toilet bowl. Once all of the water is sucked out of the toilet bowl, the water stops flowing over the trapway and the flush cycle ends. All of this happens completely by gravity. When you release the lever, the flapper returns to a closed position sealing off the tank again. Water from your supply line rushes back into the toilet tank via the *fill tube*. Water fills the toilet tank until a float rises to a particular level and shuts off the incoming water.

If your water service is interrupted, you can continue to use your toilet by filling the tank manually after a flush cycle. Flush the toilet like normal and when the flush cycle is over, just use a bucket or pot to pour water back into the tank until it reaches its normal fill level. A modern toilet will use a little over a gallon of water for each flush cycle—although older toilets can use as much as four gallons. This is probably one of the reasons you never see a real focus on how bathrooms work after the Zombie Apocalypse. As long as you have water and gravity, you will have a working toilet. By reading this book, you will be prepared to have enough water. (If for some reason gravity stops working, then you have bigger issues than this book can address.)

Don't feel like you are limited to drinking just plain water to get the hydration that you need. Most people have a good supply of beverages in their refrigerator. It is also not uncommon for someone to have a case or two of bottled water in their pantry. Take a few minutes to assess what you do have on hand. It is quite likely that you already have enough to drink in your house that you could easily last two or three days without a trip to the store. If this is not the case, then pick up a case of bottled water the next time you go to the grocery store and store it in a closet and you should be more than ready.

Food

Similar to how you probably already have enough water on hand, it is also very likely that you have sufficient food to be able to survive two to three days without a trip to the grocery store. This is a good thing, because who wants to dodge zombies while trying to run to the store for milk? Take stock of what food you have already in your house. You most likely have some canned goods and dried goods in your pantry. On top of that, you probably have some leftovers in the refrigerator waiting to be used. Any type of food that can be eaten with little or no preparation is better since you don't know what kinds of conditions you are going to encounter. Cereal, dried fruit, nuts, peanut butter—and even snacks like pretzels and chips—all have a long shelf life and can be eaten without any preparation. This matters because, depending on the circumstances, your water or power might be sporadic or even not working altogether. Canned food is also excellent for this since you can technically just eat it out of the can if necessary. Granted, this may not be the most appetizing meal but it certainly beats the alternative. Having access to canned food also means you need to have a manual can opener in case your power goes out. That also brings up an important point:

What About Your Refrigerator When the Power Goes Out?

Obviously when you lose power, your refrigerator will not run. When it is not running, that (also obviously) means anything stored inside of it will no longer be cooled. Granted, this doesn't happen immediately. A good rule of thumb is that your refrigerator will continue to keep food stored inside at a safe temperature for about four hours. The length of time can be affected by environmental conditions—if the temperature in your house is cool, then the interior of your refrigerator will stay cooler longer. Likewise, if your power goes out in the middle of summer and your house is sweltering, then your refrigerator won't safely stay cool as long. There are things you can do to help mitigate this. The USDA recommends prolonging the cooling time by placing ice in your refrigerator. If the power outage is localized and you can get to a part of town (or another town) with power, most grocery and convenience stores sell bags of ice. Several of these bags can be placed into your refrigerator to help it maintain a safe temperature inside for a longer period of time.

It also stands to reason that you should minimize the number of times you open the refrigerator door and keep the door open for as short a period of time as possible when you do open it. If you have access to ice and keeping your entire refrigerator filled doesn't seem feasible, transfer your food to a portable ice chest like you use to keep food and drinks cold in picnics. I personally have used this method to keep the better part of a refrigerator's contents cool for several days.

Now several times I have mentioned a "safe temperature." Food stored in your refrigerator is considered safe to eat as long as it remains stored below 40 °F (about 4 °C). Refrigerated food that reaches a temperature of higher than 40 °F and remains there for more than two hours (or one hour at a temperature of more than 90 °F or 32 °C) should be considered unsafe and disposed of immediately. DO NOT taste any questionable food to see if it is spoiled. You are operating under the assumption that you are going to need to be self-sufficient for a period of days. You do not need the added danger of contracting food poisoning when medical attention could be hard to come by. If there is any question as to whether food is safe to consume or not, your safest bet is to get rid of it. "When in doubt, throw it out" is the motto to live by.

Chest freezers can maintain safe temperatures for food stored inside them for a longer period of time. Freezers are typically more insulated than a refrigerator and the food stored in them (being frozen) is stored at a lower temperature. Chest freezers by design keep the cool air inside them longer. Hot air rises and cool air falls so when you open your refrigerator, the cool air inside will escape through the open door and sink down to your kitchen floor. A chest freezer has the door on the top and you access it by reaching down into it. That means that when you open a chest freezer door, the cold air will stay inside the freezer.

A chest freezer that is mostly filled will maintain a safe temperature for 24 hours whereas a freezer that is half filled or less will still maintain a safe temperature for 12 hours. Just like your refrigerator, your freezer can also be supplemented by packing it with ice. Also like your refrigerator, you should not open the freezer door unless it is absolutely necessary and then only keep the freezer door open for as short a period as possible to help maintain the internal temperature and to make the food stored inside last longer. When assessing the safety of frozen food, temperature again is key. Any frozen food item that has been kept below 40 °F or that still contains ice crystals is safe to eat (or refreeze as the case may be). Again, you should never taste-test possibly spoiled food. When in doubt, throw it out.

When planning on being partially or fully self-sufficient for 24–72 hours, the likelihood of needing to stockpile food is low. Of course you would like to be able to cook the food or at least to be able to warm it up. In the event of a natural disaster (Zombie Apocalypse or not), a hot meal can really go a long way. A camp stove or portable stove is perfect for this. Camp stoves are small, lightweight portable stoves that typically provide one or two burners to cook food on. They typically use liquid propane (LP) tanks to provide the heat. Camp stoves can be found online as well as in stores that sell camping, hunting, and outdoors supplies. They can range in price from under $50 to over $200 depending on the size of the stove and its features. For the purpose of disaster preparedness, you don't need anything too fancy since the more "bells and whistles" just means the more things that can break. You just want something that can be used to heat and prepare food, but something also small enough that you can store it when you are not using it. The LP tanks can be purchased in the same stores as the camp stoves as well as at the larger home improvement stores.

Don't rule out your grill when it comes to food preparation, either. I know of several cases where a neighborhood was without power and the residents, knowing that most of the food in their refrigerators was going to spoil, emptied their fridges and fired up their grills. They got together and cooked as much as they could and shared it around the neighborhood. When your world is upended by a disaster, sometimes the normalcy and comfort of a hot meal can really help reduce the stress of the situation. In this case, it also had the added benefit that the neighbors were able to check on each other to make sure that everyone was safe, healthy, and did not need medical attention.

Remember, you are planning on being partially or completely self-sufficient for an extended period of time. Whether it's a horde of marauding zombies or a flash flood that has closed roads, there is a very real chance that medical assistance may be unable to reach you or that they are possibly otherwise occupied. There is a survival term known as "self rescue" which means just what it sounds like—when you find yourself in a dangerous situation, you should be prepared to take measures to remove yourself from the situation and preferably without putting other people at risk to rescue you. During natural disasters there will be times where help will be unavailable to you and the only thing that will get you through the situation you are in is your skills, your wits, and your preparedness.

Disaster Preparedness Kit for Your House

At this point, we have established that you have the basic survival elements covered—you have safe shelter, you have sufficient clean water, and you have sufficient food. You are now in position to ride out the event and remain as self-sufficient as necessary for the 48–72 hours before normal services are brought back online. Naturally you still want to be as comfortable as possible throughout and not just survive. To that end, there are some things you should have on-hand in your house. It is highly recommended that you gather all of these items into one place and store them in a cool, dry place that is easily accessible. After all, you don't want to be clamoring around in your attic or a crawlspace looking for your preparedness kit in the middle of a disaster.

Store as much of this as you can in one container that is clearly marked—that way there will be no confusion if you need to tell someone else to get the disaster preparedness kit from the shelf in the laundry room, for example. Also marking the container helps keep its purpose in the front of your mind when you are cleaning and rearranging. This helps remind you to keep the kit accessible and not to shove it into the back of a closet and stack stuff on it. Once again, when the time arises that you need this—you will need it FAST.

Your disaster preparedness kit should include:

- A packet with a copy of all of your important documents (as detailed in Chapter 1). This packet should be updated once a year to ensure you have the correct information, phone numbers, account numbers, etc.
- Radio with NOAA Weather Radio—either battery operated or hand-cranked. Aside from the weather information, a radio might be your only source of news and information as well as updates on the current situation.
- Flashlights—One is good, but more than one is always better.
- Extra batteries for the radio and flashlights—batteries should be replaced annually. Technically batteries have a shelf life of longer than a year, but it's best not to press your luck.
- First aid kit—a basic pre-packed First Aid Kit will serve this purpose. Be sure you know what is in the kit and how to use it.
- Face covering—either a face mask or bandana will do. Some disasters will cause the air to be filled with smoke, dust, or other debris which is hazardous to breathe.
- Tarps or plastic sheeting—these have many uses. Tarps can be used to cover broken windows or as a "quick fix" for a hole in your roof. In a pinch, a tarp can be used as a blanket or laid on the ground to provide a dry place to sit or lie down.
- Duct tape—no disaster preparedness kit should be without this. Duct tape can be used to do anything from covering broken

windows, sealing hoses or pipes, to holding damaged doors closed. Duct tape can even be used as a bandage as a last resort.

- Moist towelettes—with no running water (or no hot water), personal sanitation is very important.
- Garbage bags—garbage bags can be used for storage, for keeping things dry, or for their intended purpose. Another very useful item to have.
- Plastic zip-ties—almost as handy as duct tape, plastic zip-ties can be a lifesaver when you need things to be held together or strapped down. They are cheap and strong.
- Multi-tool—granted you are going to be in your house with access to your tools, but having a good multi-tool in your disaster preparedness kit is always a good idea. Your tools might not be accessible when a disaster occurs and, as mentioned earlier, when you need this kit, you are going to need it fast. When seconds count, you don't want to be rummaging around in your garage trying to find a screwdriver or pliers.
- Utility shut-off tool—if you need a special wrench or tool to be able to shut off your utilities, you should definitely have one in this kit.
- Manual can opener—remember earlier when I mentioned that you likely had enough canned food to last through the disaster? Well, those cans are no good to you if you can't open them!
- Battery packs—you should have one good battery pack for each cellphone in your house. Also be sure to have the correct cable in the kit as well. These are the only things that may not need to be stored in the kit as they are only good to you when they are charged.
- Blankets—if your power goes out during the winter, be prepared for it to get chilly.
- Rain poncho, boots, work gloves—you will probably need to go outside into whatever elements are happening either to assess any damage to your house or to make any repairs. A rain poncho is essential. Sturdy boots will protect your feet from any debris on the ground while a good pair of work gloves will help protect your hands.
- Paper and writing instrument—you never know when the need might arise to label something, put a sign on your door, or provide information to someone. Keep a notepad and something to write with (I prefer either a pencil or permanent marker) in your kit at all times. They are not expensive and they

don't take up much room, but they are very valuable when you need them.

While not absolutely essential to your survival, there are some other items that prove very valuable to have handy in the case of a disaster.

- Books, magazines, activities for kids—no power means no lights and no Internet. How did we ever occupy ourselves before? Once you have your shelter secured, be prepared for a lot of downtime. You should have something to occupy your time as well as something non-powered and non–Internet related for any children you have in your house.
- Pet supplies—your pets are going to be going through the same stressful situation you are—perhaps moreso so for them since they don't know what is happening. Obviously you should plan to have enough food and water for them, but also you should be able to provide them with clean, warm bedding and treats or toys to help occupy them. Pets can provide a great deal of comfort and companionship during a crisis and your presence will provide the same for them.
- Heat—if you live anywhere that gets cold, you will definitely want some type of non-electric heat source. The good news is that there are several small space heaters on the market that use the same LP fuel as the camp stoves. While you're not going to heat your entire house with one of these, you can get one room quite comfortable. Obviously this comes with some words of caution. These space heaters produce a flame so they should NEVER be left unattended and NEVER be left to run overnight. Also, the heat is produced by burning propane which produces carbon monoxide. Carbon monoxide is a colorless, odorless gas that is a byproduct of the burning of fossil fuels. Carbon monoxide poisoning can cause headache, dizziness, confusion, drowsiness, and ultimately death. Be sure any fuel-burning heat source is only used in well ventilated areas.

Summary: How Likely Is This to Happen?

How likely is the Zombie Apocalypse to happen? It is completely unlikely. However, if you remove the zombies from the equation and think about how likely it is that you will experience some type of protracted service interruption, then your odds increase dramatically. Millions of people every year experience some type of small-scale service interruption. Maybe a strong storm moves through your area and the winds blow tree branches down onto power lines causing your power to be out for several hours. A water main could break leaving you without running water for a period of time. Most of these scenarios will only last for a few hours, but it is best to be prepared.

In early November of 2017, an unusually strong autumn storm blew through my city. The storm contained a microburst with very strong localized straight-line winds. These winds toppled trees onto dozens of power lines leading to and from the main power substation that provided power to my community. The power substation itself also sustained damage from the winds. As a result, my entire city was completely without power for nearly 72 hours while power crews from all over the state repaired the damage to the poles and substation.

Homes and businesses were dark. Grocery stores without generator backups lost their entire stock of refrigerated and frozen foods. Businesses that could remain open were limited to cash-only transactions since there was no power to their electronic credit card scanners. Traffic lights and streetlights were out. Community warming stations were set up due to the fact that this occurred in early autumn and the weather was cool—especially at night. Water pressure dropped significantly after the first 24 hours and the water that was left was obviously cold. Luckily for my family and me, the ordeal wasn't too uncomfortable. The power outage was localized to my city and both of our jobs were outside the city and so our offices had power. We could take our electronic devices and phones to work and charge them there. Our gym was also outside of the area of the power outage so we had access to showers with hot water. Still, the storm could have happened in the winter when driving was treacherous or it could have come with heavy rains that could have blocked roads or washed out bridges. It is not uncommon at all for you to be faced with a scenario in which you are forced to be partially or totally self-reliant for several days.

Chapter 3

The *28 Days Later* Scenario

28 Days Later is a 2002 zombie movie written by Alex Garland and directed by Danny Boyle. It introduces us to the concept of the "fast zombie." Where George Romero's zombies were slow and shambling, the fast zombies from *28 Days Later* are anything but. Fueled by the "rage virus," these zombies do everything at full speed so you're not just going to be able to escape from them by trotting away at a brisk jog. Even the infection rate is accelerated. A person coming into contact with just a single drop of fast zombie blood will succumb to infection within a matter of minutes. After that, they become a turbo charged killing machine driven forward constantly at full speed and fueled by pure rage and adrenaline. These new zombies are a drastic new take on the well-established zombie trope.

The movie opens with a group of radical environmental activists breaking into a facility where research is being done on chimpanzees. The research is naturally on the aforementioned rage virus. One of the activists is bitten by an infected chimpanzee. Within minutes she becomes a rage fueled zombie herself and attacks the other activists, thus starting the Zombie Apocalypse in Great Britain. Next we see Jim who awakens from a coma in a London hospital only to find the hospital without power and completely empty. He exits the hospital to find London in ruin. The Zombie Apocalypse has swept over the city and everywhere there are signs of death and destruction. Jim has his first encounter with the rage zombies and literally runs for his life. He is rescued by Mark and Selena who firebomb the zombies and take Jim to their shelter in a London Underground station.

There they fill Jim in on the gory details. The Zombie Apocalypse has happened and all of society in Great Britain has collapsed. They have no way of knowing, but they are only left to assume that a similar fate has befallen the rest of the world. Jim wants to check on his parents and convinces Mark and Selena to accompany him to his parents' house in Deptford in southeast London. They travel there only to find tragedy—both of Jim's parents have committed suicide. The group encounter the zombies again and fight their way away, losing Mark in the process.

As Jim and Selena travel back towards central London, they see lights in the window of one of the residences in Balfron Tower. They head there and meet up with cab driver Frank and his teenage daughter Hannah. Frank and Hannah have barricaded themselves in their flat and have been surviving, but they are now running very low on food and water. Frank tells them that he had heard a radio broadcast advising people to evacuate and proceed to a military blockade outside of Manchester. Left with few other options, they set out for Manchester in Frank's cab.

They arrive to find only tragedy once again. Manchester is in flames and the blockade appears to have been overrun and abandoned. Frank becomes infected through a freak accident and changes into a zombie, but before he can attack the survivors, a group of soldiers show up and kill him. The soldiers take Jim, Selena, and Hannah to a fortified estate under the command of Major Henry West. Major West turns out not to be the savior that the survivors had expected. He tells Jim that they were the ones making the radio broadcast, but their purpose behind it was not to attract survivors for the purpose of providing them safety and shelter. Instead, Major West has decided that he and his soldiers are chosen to repopulate the world. They made the broadcast in order to attract female survivors who would then be trapped there and used as breeding stock.

Jim and the women attempt to escape, but they are captured and Jim is locked in the makeshift brig. In the brig, Jim meets Farrell, one of Major West's soldiers who also didn't agree with his repopulation concept. Farrell tells Jim that he believes the zombie plague has not spread outside of Great Britain. Instead, the entirety of Great Britain has been quarantined and isolated from the rest of the world to prevent the zombie plague from spreading any further.

The next morning, Selena and Hannah are preparing for their grim fate while Jim and Farrell are scheduled to be executed. Farrell is shot, but Jim escapes amidst all of the confusion. At this point, Jim notices a plane flying overhead, thus confirming Farrell's theory that the zombie plague has not spread throughout the entire world. The soldiers had been keeping a zombie chained up for "study." Jim frees the zombie, locates Selena and Hannah, and they all flee during the ensuing chaos. They get as far as Frank's cab, only to find Major West there waiting for them. The Major shoots Jim in the stomach, but the three manage to escape while Major West meets his ultimate fate at the hands of the newly freed zombie.

In the next scene, 28 days have passed. Jim, Selena, and Hannah have taken refuge at a cottage in a remote area of Cumbria in the far northwest of Great Britain. Jim is recovering from his gunshot wound and it is shown that, after sufficient time, the zombies eventually die of starvation. The survivors see a Finnish jet fly overhead and they unfurl a large banner with the word "HELLO" on it in an attempt to signal to the pilot that there are survivors present.

Once again, not really a "feel good" movie, but the survivors again demonstrate many of the techniques and ideas that are translatable to surviving a natural disaster. Jim awakens to find himself in an unknown situation that quickly becomes dangerous so he attempts to remove himself from the area and find safety. Mark and Selena had established a makeshift shelter which afforded them relative safety and even the opportunity to defend themselves against the zombie horde—although they did lack any type of communication with the outside world. Frank and Hannah had a very safe shelter and even limited communication as Frank had knowledge of the radio broadcast. Their main problem was a simple lack of resources—they were running out of food and water and so they were forced to abandon their shelter for the ostensible safety of the blockade. Obviously this didn't turn out for the best in the film, but, generally speaking, seeking refuge in an established shelter in the event of a disaster is never a bad idea.

The important point to remember is that the scope of this movie takes place in the space of the titular 28 days or four weeks. Naturally getting the infrastructure, economy, and society back up and running in full capacity would be a long process, but the fact that the zombies would starve away in a matter of weeks serves the idea that a person who was properly prepared to remain self-sufficient for several weeks would have been able to survive this particular zombie menace (barring being bitten by a zombie, naturally).

Why is this time period important—especially since in the last chapter it was stated that 95 percent of service interruptions due to natural disasters are resolved within 48 to 72 hours? Well, while small scale disasters such as local blackouts, strong thunderstorms, blizzards, and the like are generally quick and services are restored in a fairly short time, there are a host of more serious natural disasters that can affect a larger area that can (and will) cause service interruptions that last many days or even weeks. Hurricanes, tornadoes, bands of strong storms, large scale floods, and wildfires can all damage entire neighborhoods and even whole cities. Damage to roads, power lines, water lines, and other infrastructure items on such a widespread scale can take many weeks to repair.

Most disaster response organizations (FEMA, the Red Cross, etc.) consider a plan to be self-sufficient for 72 hours to be a good beginning point. For more protracted disasters, their recommendation is that people should plan to be self-sufficient for a minimum of two weeks if you plan on sheltering in place. While this brings some new challenges to your preparedness plan, we will use the plan detailed in the previous chapter as a building block and make adjustments from there. First and foremost, don't feel like you need to accumulate multiple weeks' worth of supplies all at once. That would be time consuming and possibly expensive. My recommendation is to take the *Night of the Living Dead* Scenario and use that as a starting point. Gather your supplies and make all necessary plans to be self-sufficient for 72 hours. Once you have a feel for how that looks, take the recommendations in this chapter and slowly increase your supplies and your readiness until you can be comfortably self-sufficient for a week, then slowly grow that into two weeks. Before you know it, you will be able to sit comfortably back and not worry in the least about what radical environmental activists are doing while mucking about in labs.

First and foremost, is the Survivability Rule of 3—again, it's: A person can only expect to survive 3 minutes without breathable air; 3 hours with no weather protection; 3 days without water; 3 weeks without food.

Your personal safety is of primary importance. If disaster strikes, your first priority is to get yourself to a safe and secure shelter. Again, for the purpose of this chapter, we are assuming that you are in your house or place of residence and that you are planning on sheltering there for the duration of the event.

Shelter

Just like in any zombie movie (or weather emergency), the main focus of a safe and secure shelter is to make sure what is outside remains on the outside. In the event of an attack by the living dead, you would want to lock and secure all doors and immediately board up all windows and other methods of entry. Natural disasters can give you similar reasons to want to maintain that separation between the safety and comfort of your house and the outside elements. Strong winds from storms can bring tree branches (or whole trees) crashing down on your roof. Tornadoes and hurricanes can shatter windows from the windborne debris. Any damage to your windows, doors, or roof needs to be repaired as quickly as possible to keep the rain and other elements from doing any more damage to your property.

Also, sealing up any damaged windows and doors will help keep wild animals from getting into your house. Pests in your house can be dangerous to the inhabitants as they may carry disease. At minimum they could invade your food stores and rob you of supplies. Tarps, plastic sheets, duct tape, and the like can be used as a temporary fix to repair any damage to your house. It won't be permanent but it will likely be sufficient to keep your shelter safe until a more lasting fix can be put into place.

To repeat: as soon as it is safe for you to do so, you should check the inside of your house for any obvious damage to windows, doors, and ceilings and repair them as well as you can. This should be followed by walking the perimeter of your house and examining the outside for damage.

Once again: you should make an attempt to repair any damage you find to the best of your ability. If you find extensive damage to areas of your house (a large tree has blown down onto part of your house and caused massive damage to an exterior wall, for example), then you may find it necessary to completely abandon a room or two and move into less damaged rooms. When you need to do this, treat the entries into the damaged rooms like exterior doors and close them off using whatever supplies you have—barricades, boarding them up, or covering them with a tarp.

Water

Using the Survivability Rule of 3, your next concern should be a supply of clean water. All of the information about water in the *Night of the Living Dead* scenario still applies. Even in a power outage, municipal water systems will continue to provide water for a short period of time (roughly 24 hours is a good benchmark). It is still a valid option to fill pots, pans, bottles, or any other containers with water from the taps while you have the opportunity. Also, liquids in the refrigerator are valid options with a couple of caveats—you should avoid alcohol and caffeinated drinks. Both alcohol and caffeine are diuretics. Diuretics increase the excretion of water from the body or, in plain English, they make you go to the bathroom more frequently. This is obviously counterproductive if you are trying to prevent dehydration, so as tempting as it might be to grab some beer and ride out the disaster in a drunken stupor, that's not such a great idea on many levels—the least of which is you are going to need to keep your wits about you.

The Survivability Rule of 3 states that a person can survive 3 days without water. While this is technically true in that after three days without water you will die from dehydration, the process of dehydration is a gradual one that can cause problems well before death. The early stages of dehydration can cause fatigue, dizziness, and confusion. Any of these can be dangerous in a survival situation where you need to think clearly. As dehydration gets worse, more serious symptoms such as seizures and hypovolemic (low blood volume) shock can occur. There is a reason that access to water ranks immediately after breathable air and shelter.

As stated before, a person needs roughly one gallon of water per day to survive. It is also worth noting that this is the average amount that a typical person needs under normal circumstances. Pregnant or nursing women will need more as will children and people with some medical conditions. In hot weather this amount could easily double. Hot weather also brings with it a greater risk of dehydration and the onset of it will be quicker. Physical exertion in hot weather causes you to sweat more and sweating causes you to lose moisture from your body as it cools.

Given that the timeframe for self-sufficiency for this scenario is measured in weeks instead of days, it is safe to assume that you will quickly move past the readily available water supply and need to stockpile water. The easiest and quickest way to accomplish this is to buy bottled water and store it. Bottled water should be stored in its original containers in a cool, dark place. Stored this way, bottled water can be safely stored for up to two years. Cases of bottled water are typically sold as 24 packs of 20 ounce bottles. One gallon is 128 ounces so one case of bottled water would provide 3.75 gallons or a sufficient water supply for one person for a little over three days. To stockpile two weeks' worth of bottled water for one person would require roughly four cases of bottled water. This is not an insurmountable sum and will typically not be very expensive. To be fully prepared, however, you will want to have this stockpile in place well before disaster strikes and people start panic buying. Disasters can (and typically do) interrupt supply chains so you should expect grocery stores to run low or run out of stock of important items and it is just as likely that stock of certain items will be hard to find for days or weeks after the disaster has abated.

If you don't want the hassle or lack the storage space for that much bottled water, you can store your own water in other ways. First and foremost, be sure that you are storing your water in a sealed "food grade" container and not just in any bucket. A food grade container is a container that does not contain any chemicals that are hazardous to humans and will not transfer non-food chemicals to what is stored in it.

Food grade containers will be designated as such so there is no guesswork involved. At one point the only option for this was glass containers and glass containers are still excellent for storing water and food products although glass containers are heavy and breakable.

Recently several major manufacturers have started producing a wide variety of food grade plastic containers. These containers can be found at nearly every major retailer. Food grade containers designed specifically for storing water are being made with some very handy features like built-in spigots to make pouring the water easier and less messy (which means less waste). Some of them have even been specially designed to slide under a bed for out-of-the-way storage. Water stored in food grade containers should be replaced every six months. As you would expect, this is done by emptying the container and refilling it with fresh water.

When you purchase your food grade container, you should clean it thoroughly before the first use. Plastic containers should be cleaned with hot water and normal dish soap. Glass containers should be sterilized by rinsing them with a mixture of one teaspoon of unscented household bleach to one quart of water. Be sure to only use **unscented** bleach for sterilizing purposes since the chemicals added to bleach to give it a scent are hazardous.

Some final points on water:

- Drink first from the sources that will run out first—faucets, faucets in the lower level of your house, water in containers drawn from the faucets, liquids in the refrigerator, etc. Dip into your stockpile of stored water when it becomes necessary.
- If the water from your faucets becomes cloudy or discolored—**immediately** stop using those faucets as a water source.
- As cool and refreshing as it might look, avoid water from creeks and streams unless you have a way of purifying it. River water contains bacteria that can make you very sick unless all of the impurities have been filtered out. Water filtration methods will be discussed more in a later chapter.
- Unless you are specifically instructed to by authorities, **do not** ration your water. Dehydration is dangerous and even mild dehydration can cause symptoms that can prevent you from acting and thinking clearly. Water is best stored in your body. You have gone through the trouble of making sure you have enough water. Don't sell yourself short when you really need it.
- Stored water may taste "flat" or "off." This can generally be remedied by reintroducing oxygen into it. Simply pour it back

and forth between two clean containers a few times and it will taste better.

Food

By now you have established your family's safety, you have a secure shelter, and you have a good supply of clean, drinkable water. You're probably ready for something to eat.

Just like with water, you should eat the food first that has the shortest shelf life. Assuming that the situation you find yourself in has you without power for the duration of the event, this will first be the food that is stored in your refrigerator. I discussed in the Chapter 2 *Night of the Living Dead* Scenario methods of keeping food at a safe temperature in your refrigerator when the power goes out. Packing your refrigerator with ice and limiting the amount of time the door is open will help, but that will buy you no more than a couple of days under the best of circumstances. If your power is going to be out for weeks on end, there is nothing you can do to keep the food stored inside it at a safe temperature.

The smartest option, to avoid all of that food going to waste, is to fire up your grill (or camp stove) and cook it. I would recommend cooking everything you can. Any food you don't have an immediate need to eat or room to safely store can be shared with your neighbors. They might not be as well prepared for this disaster as you are and a little neighborly goodwill can go a long way. Check on them to make sure they are safe and not in need of immediate medical attention. Leverage their skills to help out. Are any of your neighbors doctors, nurses, or EMTs? Those are good people to know when normal access to medical attention cannot be assured. This is a two-way street, remember. If you see that one of your neighbors has a broken window due to wind-borne debris or a hole in their roof, then use the skills you have been using to keep you and your family safe and secure to help keep your neighbors safe and secure. Just like your neighbors may have different skill sets than you, they will likely have different levels of preparedness and different abilities to prepare or react. You shouldn't expect an elderly person to climb up on a ladder and nail a tarp on their roof, for example.

Canned Food

Obviously cooking and eating the food from your refrigerator and freezer isn't going to help you for long. We are fortunate that we live in a time where we have ready access to a wide variety of canned goods. On their way to supposed safety and shelter at Manchester, Frank, Hannah, Jim, and Selena stop at a grocery store and stock up on canned food and they had some sound reasoning behind that. Canned food is excellent for a survival situation (either a natural or a zombie-related disaster) as it has a remarkably long shelf life—meaning you don't have to do anything special to prevent the food inside from spoiling. Commercially canned food will remain safely edible for years as long as there is no damage to the can.

Rusted, swollen, or deeply dented cans are signs of potential problems and should be thrown out. Damaged cans can allow the growth of the bacteria *Clostridium botulinum* (C. botulinum) which causes botulism. Botulism is dangerous enough when the zombie hordes aren't rampaging the planet and you have quick access to the best medical treatment. If you do not have ready access to medical treatment, botulism can be deadly. Within 12–24 hours of eating food contaminated with the bacteria that causes botulism, symptoms will appear. Depending on how much of the bacteria you ingested, the symptoms can range from difficulty speaking or swallowing, dry mouth, facial weakness in the muscles on both sides of the face, blurred vision or double vision, drooping eyelids, nausea, vomiting, and abdominal cramps all the way to more severe symptoms like difficulty breathing and paralysis. This is not something you want to take a chance with under the best of circumstances. In a case where you don't have quick access to 9-1-1, an ambulance, an emergency room, or even a doctor, it is not difficult to imagine how this could be extremely dangerous and possibly fatal.

Canned food in intact cans can be stored for years—even decades—and still be edible according to the FDA. Granted, canned food stored for more than five years will lose nutritional value and will most likely not taste that great, but there are no intrinsic health risks from consuming canned food stored this long. A good rule of thumb is to assume that most canned food will be safe to store for 2–5 years. High-acid foods (juices, tomatoes, fruits, pickles, sauerkraut, and any other foods made with a vinegar-based sauce or dressing) can be safely stored for 12–18 months.

There are many advantages to stocking up on canned food. One great advantage is the wide variety of canned food to choose from. Nearly any type of fruit, vegetable, meat, sauce, and soup is readily available. Canned foods are great for disaster preparation because they can be eaten directly from the can. While it is true that eating cold canned food right out of the can might not be that appealing, not having to use your water supply to cook or to clean dishes can help your water supply last longer.

A major advantage is the simple fact that many people already have a good supply of canned food already sitting in their pantries. If you are in the process of building up your stockpile of supplies, it can get expensive. The fact that you probably already have several days' worth of canned food in your possession right now should help ease that expense.

Take stock of what canned food you have in your pantry. Check the dates on the cans. This is a perfect time to get rid of all those cans of things you just have around for some reason but never use. Maybe you bought a can of some special ingredient for a dish you never prepared. Maybe you have cans of stuff you bought on sale only to discover you didn't really like them. Clear out all of that stuff (because who wants to eat food you hate when you're trying to survive a zombie invasion?) and take stock of what is left. Look at what you have on hand with the idea of planning meals for everyone in your house for two or three weeks. Use that as a starting point for what you need to buy. Also, don't forget to have a manual (non-electric) can opener. Nothing would be worse than to have an army of undead on the streets outside your house, no power, a pantry chock full of canned food, and no way to open it!

MREs

Another viable option for long-term food storage are MREs. MRE stands for Meal Ready to Eat. Developed by the United States military as a much-needed upgrade to their field rations, MREs were designed to be a ration with a three- to ten-year shelf life that could be easily shipped, carried in the field, opened and consumed straight out of the package if necessary with no additional heat or water. The modern MRE was made standard issue to troops in 1986 and has served them well for many years with very few changes—most of those being an expansion of the menu options (from 12 entrees in 1986 to 24 entrees currently) and the addition in 1990 of a very convenient water activated flameless heater.

Each MRE comes in a tan plastic bag (earlier MREs were packaged in green bags—the change in color of the packaging reflects the U.S. military's change in expected deployment areas, from temperate forests to desert climates). The contents of a typical MRE will include:

- The main entree
- A side dish
- A dessert or snack (typically commercial candy or some type of fortified pastry)

- Crackers or bread
- A spread of some type (either cheese, peanut butter, or jelly)
- Powdered beverage mix (fruit-flavored drink, cocoa, instant coffee, or sport drink)
- Utensils
- Flameless ration heater (FRH)
- Beverage mixing bag (introduced since more soldiers rely on hydration packs instead of the traditional canteen—thus no canteen cup to mix a drink in)
- Accessory pack which includes:
    - ◊ Chewing gum (sugarless, sweetened with Xylitol)
    - ◊ Water-resistant matchbook
    - ◊ Napkin/toilet paper
    - ◊ Moist towelette
    - ◊ Seasonings (salt, pepper, sugar, creamer, Tabasco sauce)
    - ◊ Freeze dried coffee powder

MREs have a wide variety of main entrees available including chili, BBQ beef, spaghetti, beef brisket, beef stew, cheese tortellini, chicken stew, beef ravioli, and chicken pesto pasta. There are also vegetarian, Kosher, and Halal MRE options.

An MRE is obviously designed for someone who is performing strenuous physical activity so each MRE will provide about 1,200 calories. Unless you are doing hours of rigorous activity, eating three MREs a day is obviously not recommended. They do provide an excellent option for emergencies and can be eaten on their own or supplemented with food you have on hand from your food stores. In fact, to gain the most nutrition, it is recommended that you do supplement an MRE with other food.

Only certain types of food are suitable for the preservation process to be put into an MRE. You will find that MREs contain a lot of meat and starches, but not much in the way of fruits and vegetables. Troops in the field who consume only MREs for their nutrition have been known to develop digestive distress as a result of this. You are not likely to be in a situation where you will need to rely strictly on MREs for long-term survival, so for your body's sake you should supplement them with some vitamin-rich fruits and vegetables.

One of the most convenient additions to the MRE is the flameless ration heater (FRH). The FRH is a pouch into which a small amount of water is poured. This starts an endothermic reaction by reacting with a mixture of powdered magnesium metal, iron, and table salt. The result heats the water to boiling very rapidly. The main entree pouch of the MRE is then placed into the FRH pouch where it heats up to 100°F (or 38°C) in about 10 minutes. This is a quick, convenient way to have a hot meal with no need to waste water in cleanup. The meals can be purchased individually or by the case (12 meals) at various online stores, army surplus stores, or stores where camping goods are sold. The MREs should be stored in a cool, dark place away from direct sunlight or heat sources; they have a shelf life of 5 years when stored properly.

A suggestion if you are starting to stockpile MREs would be to purchase a few at a time—one case or even half of a case. Doing this on a regular basis will not only provide you some variety in the meals you have, but it will also cut down on the expense of having to purchase the entire supply at one time. Assuming you are going to use the MREs to supplement your other stockpile of food and only eat one MRE per day, you will still need around two cases per person to ride out an event lasting three weeks. Purchasing them over time also has the added benefit of staggering the shelf life of your stockpile. Buying all of the MREs you need to sustain you and your family could be a substantial cost if you did it all at once. Imagine having to make that entire purchase again in five years. Staggering your supply will also prevent waste. You should be checking the shelf life of your MREs regularly. When you have some that are getting close to expiring, go ahead and use them. Eat them. That's what they're for, after all! If you only have to replace one case of MREs per year, that's only twelve meals you can spread out over time instead of just having to dump your entire stock due to their being out of date.

Freeze-Dried Food

Freeze-dried food has long been a staple for hikers and backpackers. Freeze-dried food has the convenience of being light, easy to carry, quick to prepare (just add boiling water), and it has an incredibly long shelf life.

Campers, hikers, and backpackers have been voluntarily putting themselves into situations very similar to the types of events you are working to prepare for. Granted, most hikers aren't trekking through the backwoods to escape zombies—however when they do set up camp, they are in an area where there is no power or indoor plumbing and they still need to eat so they are forced to be self-sufficient. Backpackers give themselves the added difficulty that they need to physically carry all of their food and shelter with them. Naturally, hikers and backpackers have learned to travel light. They were among the first groups of people to regularly use dehydrated and freeze-dried food for exactly the reasons I described above: it's light, it's easy to carry, and it's quick to prepare.

The process of preserving food by dehydrating has been around nearly as long as humans have. There have been documented cases of Romans and early Middle Easterners preserving food by dehydrating it. It is a relatively simple process: the food is exposed to circulating hot, dry air. The air is at a hot enough temperature to remove the water from the food, but not so high as to cook the food. What remains is a food product that generally has 90 to 95 percent of the moisture content removed from it. The removal of the moisture is what prevents the growth of bacteria and what preserves the food in a shelf-stable state. The downside to dehydrating food is that the final product is generally pretty hard and (obviously) very dry—think beef jerky or banana chips. Dehydration also breaks down certain vitamins and minerals in the food so there is a dramatic reduction in vitamins A and C, thiamine (vitamin B1), riboflavin (vitamin B2), and niacin (vitamin B3)—hardly optimal when you are relying on this food for your health and survival.

The major advantage to dehydrated food is the unusually long shelf life. Stored properly, dehydrated food can last decades—25 to 30 years is not out of the question.

Freeze-drying food is a more complicated process. The food product is frozen and the pressure is lowered to the point that the ice (and thus the moisture) changes from a solid directly into a gas—a process known as sublimation. This allows for the removal of almost 99 percent of the moisture from the food, but the food still maintains its overall structure and nearly all of its vitamins and minerals (vitamin C being the main exception as it breaks down very quickly). Freeze-dried food can be reconstituted by simply adding water (hot or cold—depending on your taste) and you're left with something that looks and tastes like, well, food. To use the previous example: a dehydrated banana is a banana chip—dense, dry, and hard. A freeze dried banana with a little water added to it will look, smell, taste, and have the consistency of a banana. Add to this the fact that nearly any food can be freeze-dried including fruits, vegetables, meat, cheese, eggs, milk, cream, ice cream, cheesecake, bread, spices, herbs, and even coffee (this is what "instant coffee" is). Freeze-dried foods are also light (since they are dry), easy to store, and quick to prepare. You can have a piping hot meal by pouring hot water into a packet of freeze-dried food and stirring it around for a few minutes. Freeze-dried foods also have a long shelf life. Just like dehydrated food, properly stored freeze-dried food can be safely stored for 25–30 years without any issues.

Disaster Preparedness Kit for Your House

Just as discussed in the previous chapter, there are some supplies you should have on-hand and easily available in order to help you ride out the situation in relative ease and comfort. The disaster preparedness kit for this scenario is similar to the one described in the previous chapter, but with a few modifications for the longer time that you expect to be self-sufficient. If you already have a disaster preparedness kit in place, you can use that as a starting point and make changes as necessary.

Once again, the idea is to have the necessary supplies to be able to remain as close to fully self-sufficient as possible for two to three weeks. All of the items in the disaster preparedness kit should be gathered into one place and packed in as few separate containers as possible. They should be clearly marked as to what they are and they should be stored in a cool, dry place that is easily accessible. Just like before—when the time comes that you need this kit, you will want to be able to put your hands on it quickly. It may seem trite, but regardless of whether we're talking about a tornado, fire, flood, or attack by a roving pack of the living dead—seconds count in a disaster. You never want to be rummaging around looking for parts of your kit when a disaster is bearing down on you!

Your disaster preparedness kit should include:

- A packet with a copy of all of your important documents (as detailed in Chapter 1). This packet should be updated once a year to ensure you have the correct information, phone numbers, account numbers, etc.
- Radio with NOAA Weather Radio—either battery operated or hand-cranked. Aside from the weather information, a radio might be your only source of news and information as well as updates on the current situation.
- Flashlights—One is good, but more than one is always better.
- Battery-powered LED lanterns—with the power expected to be out for an extended period of time, battery-powered lanterns will light up a room much better than a flashlight. Lanterns with LED lights will produce a bright light and they do not use much energy, so the batteries will last longer. LED lights are also cool

to the touch so you don't need to worry about a potential heat source, fire hazard, or risk of burns.

- Extra batteries for the radio and flashlights—batteries should be replaced annually. Technically batteries have a shelf life of longer than a year, but it's best not to press your luck.
- First aid kit—a basic pre-packed first aid kit will probably not serve you well in an extended disaster. Larger, more complete kits are available for purchase, but you can just as easily build your own. A good place to start is the recommendations by the Red Cross. They suggest a first aid kit contain:
    - ◊ 2 absorbent compress dressings (5" × 9")
    - ◊ 25 adhesive bandages of assorted sizes
    - ◊ 5 packets of antibiotic ointment
    - ◊ 5 packets of antiseptic wipes
    - ◊ 2 packets of aspirin
    - ◊ 1 emergency blanket
    - ◊ 1 instant cold compress
    - ◊ 2 pair of nonlatex gloves
    - ◊ 2 packets of hydrocortisone ointment
    - ◊ 1 roll of 3" gauze bandage
    - ◊ 1 roll of 4" bandage
    - ◊ 5 sterile pads (3" × 3")
    - ◊ 5 sterile gauze pads (4" × 4")
    - ◊ 1 thermometer—oral, non-mercury, non-glass
    - ◊ 2 triangular bandages
    - ◊ 1 pair of tweezers
    - ◊ 1 emergency first aid guide
- Whistle or signal mirror—for when you need to draw attention to yourself.
- Face covering—As discussed in the last chapter, your most practical choice for a face covering is an N95 respirator mask. An N95 respirator mask will filter out 95 percent of airborne particles larger than 0.3 microns and allow you to safely breathe. Since face masks have an effective lifespan, you should keep at least one box of them on hand for you and each person sheltering with you. For most situations, an N95 face mask will provide you with all of the protection you need although your circumstances might require more protection.

    If you live downwind from a chemical processing facility or near a railroad or major highway where hazardous materials are transported, then you might be inclined to add some cartridge-based respirator masks to your preparation kit. These respirator masks can provide protection against certain chemical, biological, nuclear, and radioactive material in the air. While these respirator masks and their cartridges are more expensive than regular N95 face masks, the added protection they provide could mean the difference between safety and very serious problems. While there is no canonical evidence as to whether a cartridge-based respirator mask will protect against exposure to 2-4-5 Trioxin (as seen in the *Return of the Living Dead Part* films), the protection they provide against other chemical, biological, and radiological hazards would logically provide protection against this type of toxin as well. Although to be safe, if you ever happen to find a barrel of an unknown substance—your safest bet is to just not open it.

- Tarps or plastic sheeting—these have many uses. Tarps can be used to cover broken windows or as a "quick fix" for a hole in your roof. In a pinch, a tarp can be used as a blanket, rain poncho, or laid on the ground to provide a dry place to sit or lie down.
- Duct tape—no disaster preparedness kit should be without this. Duct tape can be used to do anything from covering broken windows, sealing hoses or pipes, to holding damaged doors closed. Duct tape can even be used as a bandage as a last resort. It clearly has a million and one uses. If you think you have enough duct tape in your kit, go ahead and buy another roll just to be safe!
- Moist towelettes—with no running water (or not hot water), personal sanitation is very important. Being able to clean yourself with moist towelettes also extends your water supply since you don't need to dip into your drinkable water for cleaning.
- Feminine hygiene products—along the line of personal hygiene, you should have a sufficient supply of feminine hygiene products for all of the women you expect to be sheltering in your house.
- Garbage bags—garbage bags can be used for storage, for keeping things dry, or for their intended purpose. They are another very useful item to have. Garbage bags and a bucket can also serve as a makeshift toilet. This also helps extend your water supply since you don't have to use your drinkable water to flush your toilet. The concept behind this works pretty much like you'd expect: line the bucket with the garbage bag, conduct your business, then remove the bag, tie it up, and dispose of it.
- Plastic zip-ties—almost as handy as duct tape, plastic zip-ties

can be a lifesaver when you need things to be held together or strapped down. They are cheap and strong. I put zip-ties in the same category as duct tape—if you think you have enough, go ahead and buy another pack.

- Multi-tool—granted you are going to be in your house with access to your tools, but having a good multi-tool in your disaster preparedness kit is always a good idea. Your tools might not be accessible when a disaster occurs and, as mentioned earlier, when you need this kit, you are going to need it fast. When seconds count, you don't want to be rummaging around in your garage trying to find a screwdriver or pliers.
- Utility shut-off tool—if you need a special wrench or tool to be able to shut off your utilities, definitely have one in this kit. A specialized utility shut-off tool is typically made of a non-sparking alloy. This is important when you factor in that you might need to shut off a leaking gas line—a situation where you obviously do not want any stray sparks!
- Manual can opener—remember earlier when I mentioned that you likely had enough canned food to last through the disaster? Well, those cans are no good to you if you can't open them! If you are looking to maximize space, the military surplus P-38 can opener will fit on a keychain.
- Battery packs—you should have one good battery pack for each cellphone in your house. Also be sure to have the correct cable in the kit as well. These are the only things that may not need to be stored in the kit as they are only good to you when they are charged.
- Blankets—if your power goes out during the winter, be prepared for it to get chilly.
- Sleeping bags—While a bed is great, sleeping bags provide some added benefit. If it is cold, a sleeping bag in your bed with extra blankets helps to add warmth. If it is hot, a sleeping bag makes it easier to sleep outside where it is cooler.
- One complete change of weather appropriate clothes—Fire, food, or Zombie Apocalypse, when it happens you are probably going to be caught unaware. Maybe you are in bed asleep when the tornado sirens go off. Maybe you were caught outside when a storm moved through. If you are stuck wearing clothes that are too hot, too cold, or too wet—that's never a good thing.
- Rain poncho, boots, work gloves—you will probably need to go outside to assess any damage to your house or to make any repairs. A rain poncho is essential in keeping you dry. Sturdy

boots will protect your feet from any debris on the ground while a good pair of work gloves will help protect your hands.

- Paper and writing instrument—you never know when the need might arise to label something, put a sign on your door, or provide information to someone. Keep a notepad and something to write with (I prefer either a pencil or permanent marker) in your kit at all times. They are not expensive and they don't take up much room, but they are invaluable when you need them.
- Paper map of the local area—while you probably know your neighborhood very well from the road or sidewalk, a paper map of the local area will come in handy. Using it will allow you to get around if the roads are impassible or if bridges are out.
- 30 day supply of prescription medicine—a protracted disaster could mean you won't have ready access to your local pharmacy or supply chain interruptions could mean your local pharmacy might not have adequate supplies. You should always have a minimum of a 30-day supply of any prescription medication that you or anyone in your household needs. Missing doses of some prescription medicines could be life threatening.
- Over-the-counter (OTC) medicine—there are several important OTC medications you should keep a supply of:
    - ◊ Aspirin—pain reliever, fever reducer, blood thinner. Aspirin can also be great to reduce muscle aches, headaches, toothaches, and even help someone recover from a heart attack or to prevent future ones. Stock both adult and children's aspirin if you have both adults and kids in your house
    - ◊ Ibuprofen—Ibuprofen serves to relieve pain and reduce inflammation and swelling. It can also reduce fever.
    - ◊ Antacids—Stress can wreak havoc on your digestive system. Ulcers can form or be made worse for those who already have them. A good supply of antacids will help alleviate this pain.
    - ◊ Antihistamines—No power means no air conditioner which means more open windows and more time outside. Anyone with seasonal allergies will know the misery of a flare up. Antihistamines and anti-allergens will help make this more bearable.
    - ◊ Bismuth subsalicylate—Pink bismuth (more commonly sold as the brand name Pepto-Bismol) is an effective treatment for indigestion, nausea, heartburn, gas, and diarrhea.

Most of those symptoms will just make you feel bad, but diarrhea can be dangerous and even deadly when left untreated. Aside from the obvious digestive issues, you will quickly become dehydrated due to the extra loss of fluids. Dehydration in a disaster situation is particularly dangerous.

  - ◊ Cough medicine—There are two major categories of cough medicine: antitussives are cough suppressants (they block the body's cough reflex) whereas expectorants thin the mucus and make it easier to clear when you cough. Both have their purposes. Someone who is sick and coughing can spread their sickness. On the other hand, being congested and unable to cough the mucus free from your lungs can lead to many dangerous conditions—including pneumonia.
  - ◊ Laxatives—Just like diarrhea can kill, constipation can also kill if left untreated. Stress coupled with foods that might be outside of your normal diet can lead to digestive distress.
  - ◊ Sleep aids—The stress of a disaster can make it difficult to sleep. Not getting enough sleep will leave a person groggy and "brain fogged" and so unable to make quick decisions or act with good judgment. This can be dangerous or even deadly in the wake of a natural disaster.
  - ◊ Saline spray—sold as a decongestant, saline solution can also be used to help irrigate wounds, flush debris from eyes, and even clean your contact lenses. Saline solution also helps moisten dry nasal passages and curb inflammation of mucous membranes.
  - ◊ Vitamins—Despite your best efforts, the food you eat to survive probably won't have the necessary vitamins. Even a basic multivitamin will help ensure you stay as healthy as you can until the disaster is over. It goes without saying that your overall health is paramount to your survival.
- Cash—Even with the power out or unreliable, there will still likely be stores open. With no power they will not be able to process credit card transactions, though. Any business open will be operating on a "cash only" basis. It is also safe to assume that widespread power outages will mean your ATM will not work. You should have some cash put aside for just this type of situation. I would recommend at least $100 in small bills.
- Paper plates and plastic utensils—coming back to the fact that we are assuming you have no running water, it only makes sense to eat your meals on disposable plates. This way you don't have to use your supply of drinkable water to wash dishes.

- Books, magazines, board games—Just think of all of the time you currently spend watching TV or on electronic devices. Obviously no power and no Internet will mean that you'll need to find something else to do to occupy your time. You will need to take into consideration any children you have sheltering with you as well. This would be a great time to have some impromptu family game nights since board games and the like just require a little bit of light and some willing players. Aside from killing time, games are a great way to relieve stress and add some feelings of normalcy back into what could be a scary situation.
- Pet supplies—a natural disaster is no less stressful on your pets. If anything, it can be more stressful for them since they have no idea what is going on. As pet owners, it goes without saying that your food and water supply should also include enough water and food for your furry companions. You should also provide them with some type of familiar setting—warm bedding, plenty of treats, and their favorite toys. Without electronics to distract you, this gives you a great chance to strengthen your bond with your pets. Having them around you, comfortable and happy, will provide you stress relief. Your pets being able to spend time with you will be a stress relief for them since you are their primary sense of normalcy.

Staying Cool with No Power

Summer in most areas means sunny, hot weather. This is great when you can enjoy it at your leisure then retreat to the comfort of an air conditioned house when it gets too hot and humid. Of course, a prolonged power outage in the summer means no air conditioner. So how do you stay cool during a power outage in the midst of the summer heat?

- Stay hydrated—you need to make absolutely sure you drink enough water when the weather gets hot. Rationing your water to make it go longer is of no benefit if you give yourself heatstroke. Plan ahead. Have plenty of water.
- Take a dip—have access to a pool? Use it. Even if all you have is a bathtub filled with water, take advantage of it. The evaporation of the moisture from your skin will help cool you down.

- Block off the hottest rooms—the rooms that face the sun are going to be the hottest rooms in your house. Cover their windows with tarps to keep the sun from beating in. If that doesn't provide enough relief, shut them off completely. Close the doors and seal them either with duct tape or by stuffing towels or rags under the door. The more you can do to keep the heat contained in those sun-facing rooms, the cooler the rest of your house will be.
- Open windows—it goes without saying, but open every window and door that you can. The more of a cross breeze you can get going, the cooler it will be.
- Sleep in the lowest part of your house—heat rises so sleeping downstairs or in a basement is going to be more comfortable than a bedroom on an upper floor.
- Sleep outside—don't rule out sleeping in the great outdoors if that is an option you can do safely. Even the warmest day can get surprisingly cool at night if you're outside under the stars.
- Battery operated fans—circulating air makes you feel cooler and there are many different choices in battery operated fans. They can be anything from small camp fans meant to hang in a tent all the way up to larger fans that can circulate air in an entire room.
- Cooling towels—there are several manufacturers who make specially designed cooling towels and bandanas. You wet them in cold water, wring them out, and then drape them around your neck. They are made of a special material that feels relatively dry even when it is damp and provides for slow evaporation. This slow evaporation of the water helps cool your skin where it is placed. Even if you don't have access to a special cooling towel, a regular towel or cloth can be used in a pinch and will deliver a similar result.
- Minimize your time outside—it's already hot enough, don't make yourself feel worse by spending too much time out in the sun. It will just serve to make you hotter and then will take that much longer to cool off. Any work you need to do outside should be put off as much as possible until later in the day.
- Cook outside—you're probably already cooking your meals on a grill or camp stove. Move the stove outside so as not to heat up the room.
- Don't cook unless you have to—while a hot meal is great, sometimes you want to remain as cool as possible. If the weather is hot, you probably won't be in the mood for piping hot food

anyway. Most emergency food can be eaten cold. MREs can be eaten directly out of the package whereas freeze-dried meals can be reconstituted with cold water and canned food can be eaten cold right out of the can.

- Battery powered lights instead of candles—aside from the safety element, having an open flame inside will put heat into a room. It might not seem like much, but a few candles can affect the overall temperature of a room. Battery operated lights—specifically LED lights—provide light without adding heat.

Staying Warm with No Power

A disaster is just as likely to strike in the dead of winter. Snow, sleet, sub-zero temperatures, and blustery winds are one thing when you just have to deal with them long enough to get inside into the heat. No power means no heat and a house, no matter how well insulated, will start to cool down very quickly in the winter when the heat goes out.

- Dress in layers—the easiest way to keep yourself warm is to wear layers of clothes. A couple of pairs of wool socks with shoes; thermal underwear under jeans with sweatpants over them; a thermal undershirt under a long sleeved shirt under a hoodie with a jacket on over that; knit caps with earmuffs; gloves with mittens on over them. Multiple layers of clothes will keep you much warmer than just one layer.
- Stay dry—if you do have to go outside into the snow, change out of your wet clothes as quickly as you can once you're back inside. Being cold and wet can quickly lead to hypothermia which can be deadly if left untreated. Signs of hypothermia include shivering, feeling tired, confused, trouble concentrating, trouble using your hands, and slurred speech. Hypothermia is dangerous under perfect conditions and can be life threatening during a natural disaster when you may not have the ability to get the necessary medical attention.
- Blankets—cover yourself with the warmest blankets you have. Don't forget about comforters from your bed or sleeping bags. They can also provide warmth.
- Limit your space—close off the coldest rooms in your house. These will generally be the rooms that face the wind. Close the vents in those rooms. Use plastic sheeting and duct tape to

seal the windows. Close the doors and seal around them using either plastic sheeting, duct tape, or rags stuffed into the cracks. Sealing off the coldest rooms will help limit the amount of cold outside air that gets in. Limit yourself to a room or two and preferably a smaller room at that. Small spaces are quicker to heat and easier to keep warm. Cool air settles so a basement or a room on your lowest level is probably not a good idea. A large dining room with a vaulted ceiling is not a good idea, either. A normal sized bedroom is ideal.

- Move around—exercise warms you up. It doesn't have to be anything overly complicated or strenuous, but just doing a few minutes of some basic exercise will provide you with some warmth. Plus, being active is always preferable to being sedentary—especially in a survival situation.
- Space heaters—there are a variety of space heaters that burn fuel ranging from LP (liquid propane) to kerosene. Any of these will warm up a small space to a comfortable level, but you should always use caution when using them. First and foremost, these heaters produce a flame so they should NEVER be left unattended and absolutely NEVER be left to run overnight. Burning fossil fuels produces carbon monoxide—an odorless, colorless gas that can be deadly and its symptoms can sneak up on you quickly. It starts with headache and dizziness and then causes confusion and drowsiness and ultimately death. Any space heater should be used in an area with adequate ventilation. It also is important to note that space heaters have surfaces that can get quite hot so there is a risk of burns and a potential fire hazard.
- Fireplace—if you have a wood-burning fireplace, this is a perfect use for it. Just like a space heater, you should never leave your fireplace unattended or burning while you sleep. You can also take bricks or large rocks and put them into the fire to heat up, then (after carefully taking them out of the fire) wrap them in towels or blankets and position them around your room to provide some long-lasting radiant heat.
- Car heater—as long as your car is not shut up in your garage, you can always sit in your car while it runs and warm up some. Obviously this is only practical while you have enough gas to run your car. Again, never do this if your car is in your garage. A running car produces carbon monoxide in its exhaust and that can quickly build up to fatal levels in an enclosed space.
- Warm food and drinks—you are already prepared enough to

have a supply of food and drinks and the ability to warm them up. Eating or drinking something warm is a great way to keep warm. Room-temperature food is not optimal, but better than nothing. Cold food and drinks will have the opposite effect and cool you down.

- Body heat—if you have family members with you, then snuggle up! Body heat does a great job of keeping you warm. Don't feel like you have to limit this to just people. Your pets will also be chilly and they'll certainly appreciate the chance to snuggle up next to you under a warm blanket.
- Avoid alcohol—as tempting as it may seem, alcohol only makes you *feel* warm. In fact, it will lower your core temperature and push you closer to hypothermia. This is aside from the effect of dulling your senses. You are in a survival situation and you need to keep your wits about you.
- Run a little water—as a precaution, you should have a trickle of water running in the lowest faucet in your house. This will help prevent your water pipes from freezing. Frozen pipes can cause a great deal of damage since water expands when it freezes. Frozen pipes can burst and then you'll have a flooded house to deal with once things get warm again.

Summary: How Likely Is This to Happen?

While the vast majority of service interruptions caused by natural disasters are resolved in a matter of hours, more widespread events do more damage and spread the damage over a broader area which means it will naturally take longer for crews to be able to repair the damage and get your services up and running again. Large-scale natural disasters such as wildfires, large tornadoes, or hurricanes can affect whole neighborhoods or even entire cities. The sheer amount of damage will make cleanup and service restoration take some time. When Hurricane Isabel worked its way up the Eastern Coast of the United States in 2003, many cities and communities suffered extensive damage. The city of Hampton, Virginia, reported that most of the city was completely without power for two weeks. Hampton has a population of nearly 140,000 people so this was not an insignificant event.

Chapter 4

The Walking Dead Scenario

The Walking Dead is a popular television show on the AMC network which, at the time of this writing, had just broadcast its eleventh and final season. It is based on a comic book series of the same name published by Image Comics and written by Robert Kirkman. The comic book series ran for a total of 193 issues and was published between 2003 and 2019.

Both the television show and comic book are centered around Rick Grimes. Rick is a sheriff's deputy who is injured in the call of duty and rushed to the hospital where he slips into a coma. He awakens from the coma to find his world radically changed. The Zombie Apocalypse has occurred while Rick was unconscious and he discovers the hospital to be without power and abandoned while showing signs of a great struggle having taken place. Encountering some "walkers" (*The Walking Dead* is another zombie property that never actually uses the word "zombie"), Rick flees the hospital only to find more death and devastation in the city outside.

The comic book series and the television show follow Rick's journey through the zombie-infested world. He eventually locates his wife Lori, his son Carl, and friend and fellow police officer Shane. They also find other small groups of survivors who then set out to make their way into the new and radically changed world. They encounter other groups of people—some with good intent and others with evil intent. They find settlements of people along the way who have even started to rebuild the rudiments of life as it was known before the Zombie Apocalypse. I won't give anything away about the ending, but suffice it to say that this scenario is THE Zombie Apocalypse. Rick and the survivors find themselves in a world in which all signs of modern civilization are gone. Cities and nations are no more. All modern comforts are gone—no power, no running water, no Internet, no radio, no grocery stores, no cars. A majority of the world's population is dead and now walk the ruined earth seeking nothing more than to devour human flesh. This is officially End of the World as We Know It territory. The *Night of the Living Dead* Scenario (Chapter 2) was designed to make you prepared to be self-sufficient for up to 72 hours (not after the total collapse of civilization). The *28 Days Later* Scenario was designed to make you prepared to be self-sufficient for up to two weeks. This chapter takes your preparation to the next logical level in that it will make you prepared to be partially or fully self-sufficient for four or more weeks. This may seem overly dramatic, but large-scale disasters (hurricanes, earthquakes, large tornadoes) can create enough widespread devastation that areas ravaged by these disasters can be without regular services for weeks on end.

The methods by which you prepare yourself are going to be familiar. The items that you prepare with will also be familiar—although with some modifications. The biggest difference is the simple fact that it is going to be difficult (if not impossible) to fully prepare and stockpile enough supplies for you and your family to be completely self-sufficient for four weeks. I will provide you with the guidelines on how to prepare and stockpile, but this scenario will also concentrate on methods of renewing your stock assuming you won't have ready access to utilities, your local grocery store, or Amazon.

Personal Safety

In *The Walking Dead*, Rick wakes up from a coma and finds himself alone in an abandoned hospital. He assesses the situation to determine his safety. Encountering some zombies, he quickly leaves the hospital and begins looking for a safe shelter. This is Survival 101: are you safe and secure where you are? If not, you need to find a place where you can be. Rick's next immediate thoughts were of the safety of his wife and son. Once he located them in a group of survivors, their focus became directed towards keeping the group safe from zombie attacks while providing them with food and water. None of these steps should seem unusual to you by this point in the book as these are the basic skills of surviving a natural disaster.

First and foremost, the Survivability Rule of 3 always comes into play. A person can survive: 3 minutes without air; 3 hours without sufficient shelter; 3 days without water; 3 weeks without food.

Breathable air is foremost on the list, but equally important is your immediate personal safety. If you are in a situation where the air is unbreathable because of smoke, dust, fumes, or the like, then you need to immediately extract yourself from that area. Likewise, all of your planning is for naught if you don't take your personal safety into consideration. If you are being attacked by the living dead, in a burning room, in the path of a flash flood, or outside during a tornado, your primary goal is to get to some type of safe shelter. For the purpose of all of the information so far, this safe shelter has been your house.

Shelter

Once you have shelter, your next immediate concern is to make it secure. It does you no good to lock yourself in a house if the zombies can just break through the windows. Likewise, if your house is damaged by the disaster, you need to make any necessary repairs to keep your dwelling habitable. That is going to be your primary shelter after all. Board up broken windows. Patch up roof damage with plywood (if possible) or a tarp (if necessary). If rooms are too damaged to make effective repairs, then close them off and consolidate yourself in the remaining parts of your house. Every effort should be made to keep the elements of the outside world on the outside of your house. This obviously applies to the weather since water or snow getting in through a damaged roof will only cause more damage. Likewise, wind blowing in through broken windows will just make it that much harder to keep your dwelling space warm in the winter or cool in the summer.

This goes beyond the elements, though. A natural disaster doesn't just disrupt human lives—wildlife will find their habitat damaged or destroyed as well and they will be seeking the same things that you are: water, food, and shelter. Unsecured doors or windows are an open invitation for critters to invade your house. Once inside, they could raid your supplies of food. They could also carry disease or their bites could be dangerous. None of these are situations you want to be in so seal up any broken windows, cracks, or holes in your structure. Let Mother Nature take care of the local fauna.

In this type of survival situation, it is also good to keep in mind whether you want people to know that your house is occupied. Generally, emergency personnel sweep through disaster affected areas as soon as they safely can looking for survivors. You will naturally want to let them know that you are there and that you are safe. However, it could take several days for the situation to calm down to the point that rescue crews can even make it into the area. Human nature being what it is, it is not unheard of for looters to make their way through neighborhoods after disasters as they assume (and rightfully so) that the police will be occupied in other areas or just simply not able to get there. Depending on the disaster and the area affected, you will need to decide whether it is smarter (and safer) to let anyone and everyone know that your house is occupied or whether it makes more sense to hide your presence.

If you are keeping your presence low-key you will need to minimize the time you spend outside, for obvious reasons. Any windows in the areas where you are staying should also be completely covered. Simply boarding them up will not be sufficient since any light source you have will be visible through the cracks. This may not seem like such a big deal, but when an entire neighborhood is dark, one house with a light in it is very noticeable! You will need to keep in mind that areas without power are usually very quiet and still. Any unusual actions will draw attention. The noise from boarding up windows or patching a leaky roof will reverberate through the neighborhood. Smoke from fires (either for heat or clearing debris) will be visible for a long way. The scent of food cooking can possibly attract more than just wildlife.

If you are planning on staying hidden, it will require some extra planning. Naturally you will want to make your presence known to emergency personnel when they come around. If the disaster is widespread enough, some of the first emergency personnel you will likely encounter will be groups going house by house checking for survivors, casualties, and potential hazards in the houses. These are the people you want to know that you are home.

Once you are safe and you have secured your shelter, you should initiate your Family Emergency Communication Plan. You need to know where each member of your family is, if they are safe where they are, and if not, where they are going. Hopefully your family will either be with you by this point or on their way to you, but circumstances could arise where this is not practical. In those cases, family members not present with you will have to rely on the training and education they received from you for just such a situation. They will need to keep an open line of communication with you until you have determined that they are somewhere safe and they have what they need to remain self-sufficient for as long as necessary. Even if they need to stay at work or school for a night or two and then make their way home, that is much wiser than risking their safety traveling home through a dangerous situation.

Water

Building on previous scenarios, you should still always use the drinkable water you have on hand and easily accessible first—that being water from your municipal water supply, liquids already in your refrigerator, etc. Once those run out, begin using any stockpiled water you have. Given that this scenario is assuming you are not going to have access to clean drinking water for at least four weeks, you will probably reach the limit of what is feasible for you to stockpile. If you remember, an average person needs about one gallon of water per day so four weeks' worth of water would be 28 gallons. If you have two people in your household, that number doubles to 56 gallons. As you can see, this would quickly become difficult to effectively store. At a certain point, it becomes more feasible to store a reasonable amount of water in your house and then look at outside sources for the remainder. The most logical outside source would be any natural source of fresh water—creeks, rivers, streams, lakes, reservoirs, etc. Keep in mind, these are **natural** sources; the chemicals in swimming pool water of course make it unsafe to drink.

Rainwater is a safe and easy option and it is also plentiful (provided you live in an area of the country that's not arid). Rainwater can be easily collected by just setting containers outside while it is raining. In *28 Days Later*, Frank and Hannah attempt to collect rain water by covering the roof of their apartment building with pots and pans. Anything that can hold water can be used—pots, pans, buckets, etc. Even spreading a tarp on the ground can be an effective method of collecting rainwater. A 10' × 12' tarp laid flat on the ground during a rain shower with just 1" of precipitation will collect close to 72 gallons of water! The rain obviously falls on your house as well. This precipitation will run down your roof into your gutters then into your downspouts. From there, most houses have their downspouts emptying into the ground.

Running your downspouts into a container can provide you with an excellent supply of drinkable water. A roof with 1,000 square feet of surface area will collect over 500 gallons of water during a 1" rainfall. A larger roof or more precipitation will provide more water, obviously. If you have the ability, you can install rain collection barrels as permanent additions to your downspouts. This will help provide you with a continually refreshing source of drinkable water. If your area of the country gets 10" of total rainfall during the spring and summer, that is over 8,000 gallons of water that is falling from the sky!

It is worth noting that rainwater is naturally very clean since it is distilled (see below for an explanation of distillation), but rainwater collected from your roof should be filtered and purified since it came into contact with several surfaces along the way before you could collect it (the shingles on your roof, the inside of your gutters, the inside of your downspout, etc.).

Once you have secured a source of natural fresh water, it is imperative to remember **never** to drink that water without purifying it. It may look crystal clear and refreshing, but the water from most rivers, streams, and creeks have bacteria in them that can make you very sick and that is not what you need when you can't get to a doctor or hospital! Water can be made safe to drink relatively easily, though.

Any water that you draw from a river, stream, or lake could have some sediment in it—especially if it has recently rained. You will want to remove the sediment or any other large particulate matter before going any further in the process of purification. To accomplish this, pour the water through a clean cloth or coffee filter. This will filter out the larger particles in the water leaving only the microscopic ones to worry about for further purification methods.

Boiling

This is one of the easiest methods of purifying water. Simply take the water and heat it up to a rolling boil. Just for the sake of clarity: water is considered to be boiling when bubbles begin to form on the bottom of the container and rise to the surface. Continued application of heat to boiling water will bring it to a *rolling boil*—which is where large bubbles are vigorously rising and breaking the surface to the point that the water itself is churning in the container. Allow it to boil this way for one full minute, then remove it from the heat, let it cool, and it is completely safe to drink. Naturally some of the water will boil away in the process and it will take some time—possibly 20–30 minutes to bring one gallon of water to a rolling boil. This could get time consuming if you were trying to purify enough water for several people. The main advantage to this method is its simplicity—all you need is water and heat.

Water purified this way can tend to taste "flat." This is due to lower levels of oxygen in the water after boiling. Fixing this is as simple as pouring the purified water back and forth between two containers. This helps re-oxygenate the water and will improve the taste dramatically.

Water Purification Tablets

These handy little items are just what they sound like—they are tablets that you drop into a container of water, shake it up, and let it sit. After a period of time, they will kill off any bacteria in the water making it safe to drink. There are several different brands of these on the market. They all have similar chemicals in them (usually chlorine, iodine, and chlorine dioxide). When the tablets are dissolved in water, they start a chemical reaction that renders the water unsuitable for bacteria, parasitic protozoans, and viruses. All of these nasty elements die off and are rendered harmless so the water is then perfectly safe to drink.

Water purification tablets do have some drawbacks, though. First off, they are not all created equal. While most of them will kill many of the microscopic nasties in stream water, not all water purification tablets will kill Cryptosporidium. Cryptosporidium are microscopic parasites that can cause some bad gastrointestinal problems if ingested.

Water purification tablets also take time to work. Some of them need up to four hours to fully purify one liter of water. Finally, some brands of water purification tablets will leave the water with a chemical taste and smell that some people find off-putting. These are definitely a "try before you buy" option—meaning, it is a good idea to sample a few different brands to see which ones (if any) are palatable to you. The last thing you want is to not drink enough water because the water purification tablets you stocked up on make your water taste bad!

Bleach

Chlorine is one of the ingredients in water purification tablets. Chlorine is also one of the active ingredients in common household bleach (specifically: sodium hypochlorite). This means you could purify water just using bleach. To purify water with bleach you first need to make sure you use ONLY household bleach that contains 5.25 percent to 6.0 percent sodium hypochlorite (the label will state this amount). NEVER use scented bleach, "color safe" bleach, bleach with added cleaners, laundry bleach, or pool chlorine for purifying water!

Purifying water with bleach is a very simple process—you simply add eight drops of bleach for every gallon of water in the container, stir it around a little bit, then let it set for 30 minutes. At the end of 30 minutes, the water should have a faint smell of chlorine. If it does not, then add another eight drops of bleach per gallon of water, stir it around, then let it sit for another 15 minutes. If, at the end of this process, the water tastes too much like chlorine for your palette, you can transfer the purified water to a new container and let it sit (uncapped) for several hours. You can also pour the water back and forth between two containers. Either of these processes will help to speed up the evaporation of the chlorine from the water which affects the taste.

Distillation

While boiling, water purification tablets, and chlorinating with bleach will remove most microbes, viruses, and parasites in water, they don't remove every type of contaminant. Distillation is the only method of purifying water that will remove microscopic particles as well as heavy metals, salts, and other chemicals. At its core, distillation is a very simple process. It is simply boiling the water, collecting the vapor as it boils off, and condensing it back into drinkable water. This can be done by various methods, but the most rudimentary method is:

- Fill a large pot about halfway with water.
- Place a baking rack in the bottom of the pot.
- Place a glass bowl in the pot. It should float on the surface of the water. The baking rack will keep it from coming into contact with the base of the pot. Make sure there is sufficient room around the sides and top of the bowl for air to freely circulate. The bowl should be large enough in diameter that it takes up most of the inside of the pot, not so large that it touches the edges of the pot.
- Place the pot lid inverted on the top of the pot. Place some ice cubes on the top of the inverted lid to help the water condense more quickly.
- Boil the water and monitor the ice on the lid. Replenish the ice as necessary.
- As the water boils, water vapor will rise up and begin to condense on the overturned lid. As it cools and condenses back into water, the water will run down the slope of the lid and drip down into the glass bowl.
- After all of the water in the pot has boiled away, condensed on the inverted lid, and dripped back into the bowl, the process is complete and the bowl is now filled with distilled water.

As you can imagine, this is a time consuming process that doesn't produce a large volume of water. Distillation should only be used as a last resort when your only sources of water are very dubious and you don't have access to the other methods of purification.

Water Filtration Systems

Dedicated water filtration systems are also a viable option. These can be as small as a one-person filtration straw or as large as multi-gallon filtration tanks. They work on the same principles as methods described above. They all have some type of element or cartridge that contains a chemically treated filter coupled with activated carbon. The chemicals will kill off bacteria and viruses while the filter will strain out debris, protozoa, and bacteria. The activated carbon can reduce contaminants like pesticides, but its primary function is to remove unpleasant tastes.

Water filtration systems work in three major ways: pump filters, gravity-fed filters, and ultraviolet purifiers. Pump filters act by using a manually operated pump mechanism to draw water from a water source and force it through the filtering element. As long as you are providing the pumping, you will be getting a supply of purified water. The biggest disadvantage to this type of system is the labor involved in filtering the water. When you stop pumping, it stops working.

Gravity-fed filtration systems are typically larger than pump-fed filtration systems. A gravity-fed system will usually hold multiple gallons of water. In this system, you pour the unfiltered water into a tank on the top of the system. Gravity will pull the water downward through the filtering element located near the middle of the system and purified water will collect in a tank at the bottom. This is not as labor intensive as a pump filter system, but it can take longer to work, as you are limited by the amount of time it takes for the water to work itself down through the filtering element.

Gravity-fed filtering systems are perfect for houses since they are larger and less portable. Their nature makes them more of a "set it and forget it" system since you will generally fill them up at night to have purified water ready for you in the morning.

Both pump filters and gravity-fed systems rely on filtering elements or cartridges to perform the filtering functions. These elements will get clogged up with use and become less efficient (i.e., they will take longer or require more effort to pump them) and will either need to be replaced or cleaned regularly.

Ultraviolet (UV) water purifiers use an ultraviolet light that is submerged into the water and activated. The UV light will run for a minute or two and that is all you need to purify the water. This system has a few drawbacks, though. First, it only works effectively on clear water—any cloudy or murky water will need to be filtered first. Secondly, these systems are typically designed for smaller containers (portable water bottles, etc.). Larger quantities of water would need multiple UV treatments to purify them fully. Finally, these systems run on batteries which may be more useful in a natural disaster to power your lights or radios.

My recommendation would be a gravity-fed water filtration system for your house and smaller ones for situations where you need to be more mobile (more about this in Chapter 5).

Food

Your next concern should be ensuring that you have an adequate supply of food—enough for you, all of the members of your family, and any pets to easily survive for four weeks or more. In the same vein as previous examples, you are going to simply build on the foundations you already have in place. Once again, this scenario will rely on your existing stockpiles as well as exploring options to consistently renew your supplies.

As in previous chapters, you should always begin by eating the food you have that will go bad first—prepared food, food in your refrigerator, food in your freezers. Those stockpiles of food are already there so there is no use in letting them go to waste. Once you have depleted those supplies, you should begin to use food that has a longer shelf life—canned food, MREs, dehydrated food, and freeze dried food. These foodstuffs have shelf lives of years (or even decades) if stored properly. That seems pretty thorough. How can we add to that? As I mentioned, a focus of this chapter is the ability to renew your existing supplies.

First off is a simple expansion of what you probably already have in your pantry—dried goods. Check your pantry for the below items and gradually add stock each week as you make your normal trips to the grocery store. Before you know it, you will have enough dried goods to last several weeks.

- Powdered milk—milk is loaded with calcium and vitamin D (good for strong bones) and a great source of potassium. It is also a good source of vitamin A (good for vision and immune health), vitamin B (responsible for energy production), vitamin C, and vitamin E (good for the skin and to help prevent cell damage). Powdered milk can also be used for cooking or just added to your coffee. You can even add powdered milk to water and stir to make a drink that tastes reasonably close to real milk. Regular milk needs to be refrigerated and still will spoil in a matter of weeks. Powdered milk is shelf stable and, according to the USDA, can be stored indefinitely. You probably already have a small box of powdered milk for cooking. The next time you are at the store, pick up a larger one (or two).

- Powdered drink mixes—coffee, tea, Ovaltine, Tang, Kool-Aid, and the like. Let's face it, who wants to drink plain water all the time?
- Bouillon cubes—bouillon cubes are small cubes of dried and seasoned stock with a touch of fat thrown in to hold it together. The word comes from the French verb "*bouillir*" which means "to boil" and you can make a very simple broth by doing just that—adding a bouillon cube to boiling water. The result is a clear, seasoned broth of beef, chicken, or vegetables. The broth can be eaten to help keep you hydrated and nourished if you are sick. Who hasn't had chicken soup to help recover from a cold? Bouillon cubes can also be added to other dishes to add flavor and savoriness. Rice, beans, vegetables, potatoes—nearly any dish can be enhanced by tossing some bouillon cubes in while you are preparing it. Bouillon cubes are also inexpensive and have a long shelf life.
- Hard cheeses encased in wax—while most of us are used to storing cheese in the refrigerator, wax-sealed cheeses (Parmesan, swiss, gouda, and the like) can be stored at room temperature for up to 25 years. The wax serves two purposes—it seals the moisture inside the cheese wheel and it also prevents the growth of bacteria (which causes the cheese to mold). Of course, this is assuming that the wax seal is intact. Once you remove the wax seal or cut into the cheese, then it becomes susceptible to mold at the normal rate.
- Pasta—dried pasta is an excellent food source. It is inexpensive to purchase and easy to store and quick to prepare. When stored properly (in an airtight container in a cool, dark place) dried pasta can remain good for several years. Pasta also comes in a wide range of shapes, sizes, and varieties so feel free to stock up.
- Dried beans—beans are another great food source for emergency preparedness. Beans have a high nutritional value providing you with calories, protein, and carbohydrates. Dried beans are easy to find—practically every grocery store stocks them. In fact, some grocery stores will sell dried beans in 25 pound bags! They should be stored in an airtight, food-grade container and the container should be kept in a cool, dark place. Properly stored, dried beans will remain edible for up to 30 years.
- Dried rice—just like dried beans, dried rice is inexpensive and easy to find. Stored the same way as dried beans, dried

rice should also last for about 30 years. Rice also provides a nutritious addition to any meal. Rice can be mixed with beans or eaten as a side dish. One important point is that only white rice can provide you with this long shelf life. Brown rice still has the husk on it and the husk has natural oils in it that will cause brown rice to spoil quicker than white rice which has the husk removed. White rice can be stored for about 30 years whereas brown rice will only last 12 to 18 months even when stored properly. Rice can also be purchased in bulk. If your local grocery store doesn't carry anything larger than boxes or small bags of rice, check at specialty Asian or Indian grocery stores. You will most likely be able to find large bags of rice there.

- Oats—dried oats (Rolled oats, Steel-cut oats, Quick-cooking oats, or plain instant oatmeal) are another good staple food product to have. Oats are a good source of protein and healthy fats. They can be cooked and eaten by themselves or they can be boiled with meats, vegetables, or fish for a hearty stew. Since they are naturally dried to less than 10 percent moisture content, they can be properly stored for 30 years. Oats are another food product that is inexpensive and easy to find. Oats come in a wide variety of strange sounding styles. The differences between the most popular kinds aren't that dramatic, though. All oat products start from the same place—the oat groat. When oats are harvested, the outer husk is removed from the oat kernel and what remains is the oat groat. The oat groat is then made into oat products with the main difference being the amount of processing that goes into it.
    - ◊ Steel Cut Oats—Steel Cut oats are oat groats that are cut into pieces. They generally have a tough texture before they are cooked. Steel Cut oats cook in 20 to 30 minutes and produce an oatmeal that has a chewier texture than oatmeal made with Rolled or Instant oats. Oatmeal made from Steel Cut oats is often referred to as Irish Oatmeal. Steel Cut oats are the least processed of the oat products.
    - ◊ Rolled Oats—Rolled oats or Old Fashioned oats are flat and flaky. They absorb more water and thus cook quicker than most other kinds of oats—cooking completely in about 5 minutes. Rolled oats are what is typically used in cookies, muffins and granola bars. Rolled oats are made by steaming the oat groats and rolling them flat. They are processed slightly more than Steel Cut oats.

- ◊ Quick Cook Oats—Quick Cook oats are, as the name implies, made to be prepared quickly. They can be cooked thoroughly in about one minute on the stove or they can also be cooked in a microwave. Quick oats are processed more than Rolled oats. The oat groats are steamed for a longer period of time, then they are rolled and cut into smaller, thinner flakes.
- ◊ Instant Oats—Instant oats are simply Quick Cook oats that have been more finely chopped. Instant oats are usually found as individual oatmeal packets designed to be microwaved. The oatmeal they produce is the softest in texture of any of the above oatmeals. Consequently, Instant oats are the most processed oat product.

- Powdered Peanut Butter—peanut butter is a staple in most people's pantries and for good reason. It is tasty and packs a lot of protein and magnesium. Peanut butter also contains omega-6 which has been shown to lower LDL (bad) cholesterol. Unfortunately, peanut butter does not have a very long shelf life. A jar of peanut butter can only be safely stored for six to nine months unopened and a mere two to three months after opening. A fairly recent trend on the market has been the introduction of powdered peanut butter, which is made by roasting peanuts and then pressing them to remove most of the oil and grinding what remains into a fine powder. It can be used in powdered form in recipes or you can add some water and reconstitute it back into peanut butter. Removing most of the oil means the remaining product is more nutritious, having about 85 percent less fat, but still nearly all of the protein and fiber. Another benefit is that powdered peanut butter can be safely stored for 4 to 5 years if the container is unopened or one year if opened.
- Honey—honey can be used as a sweetener for food or drinks. You can also eat a spoonful of honey to give you a natural energy boost. Honey is very unique in that it has no "use by" date. Honey is both low in water and high in sugar so bacteria cannot survive in it. Stored in a closed jar, honey will never spoil. In 2015 some archaeologists were excavating a tomb in Egypt. Inside the tomb they found jars of honey that had been interred there for more than 3,000 years. They took samples and found the honey to be perfectly edible. Stored honey will take on a "cloudy" appearance after a while. This is natural. This is just the crystallization of sugar in the honey. Crystalized honey is still

edible, but you can liquify it again by placing the jar (with the lid off) in hot water for a few minutes.

- Flour—flour is an essential item for baking. Compared to many of the other items mentioned, flour has a relatively short shelf life. Stored in the paper bags that you purchase it in, it will only remain good for a few months. Flour stored in an airtight container will remain good for about one year. Flour stored in an airtight container and put into a freezer will stay good for an extended period of time, however. One method of supplementing your supply would be to store a few containers of flour in a freezer while having more in airtight containers in your storage pantry. Rotate through (or use) the flour from your storage pantry while saving the frozen flour for an emergency. If you lose power for an extended period of time, your freezer will be of no use to you anyway. That would be the time to start using the frozen flour (once you allow it to come to room temperature). Granted, while flour can only be stored for about a year, consuming out-of-date flour will most likely not make you sick. Anything you bake with expired flour won't taste as good as with fresh flour, though. Flour will begin to smell "off" when it expires. If you have stored flour that develops a particularly bad or rancid smell, you should discard it immediately.
- Salt and sugar—while on the subject of cooking essentials, both salt and sugar can be stored indefinitely if stored properly.
- Yeast—fresh yeast needs to be refrigerated and even then will only last about three weeks. Dry yeast (active dry and instant yeast) will remain good for up to three years. Yeast doesn't really "go bad" or spoil like many other food products do. Yeast is made up of microorganisms with a finite lifespan. Yeast won't spoil, but the microorganisms can die, rendering the yeast ineffective. If you ever have any concerns about the viability of yeast you are using, there is a quick test to see if it is still good: dissolve 1 teaspoon of sugar in ¼ cup of warm water and add a packet of yeast. In 10 minutes, the mixture should foam up to twice its original size if the yeast is still active. Anything less means the yeast has lost its potency.
- Cooking oil—regardless of the type of oil, most cooking oils will keep for about 6 months if the bottle has been opened. Unopened bottles will stay fresh for up to three years. As far as cooking oils are concerned, glass bottles or metal tins provide a longer storage window than plastic bottles. Plastic bottles are

not completely airtight and so will let oxygen in over time, and that will accelerate the rancidity process and make the oil go bad faster. Tiny holes will form in the plastic bottles over time allowing the oil to leak out. The last thing you want is for your storage pantry and its supplies to be ruined by leaking cooking oil.

As you can see, you probably have most (if not all) of these items in your home already. These items are readily available and inexpensive enough that you can slowly increase your supplies by just picking up an additional one or two items each time you shop for groceries. Before you know it, you will have your supply pantry stocked up to the point that you can easily wait out four weeks or longer without having to make a trip to the grocery store and being self-sufficient in the process.

Safe Food Storage

Many times I mentioned "proper storage" of food items, but what does that mean exactly? Food should always be stored in a food-safe container—either mylar bags or a food-grade bucket. "Food grade" means that the container is not made with any known toxic materials and that the material the container is made from will not find its way into the food stored inside it. Food grade containers will be clearly marked so there is no confusion. Pack the food products as tightly as you can into the containers. The idea is to get as much of the air out as you can. The germs, bacteria, and microbes that get into your food and cause spoilage need oxygen to do their work. Less oxygen means less chance of spoilage.

The overall temperature of your storage area is important, too. Extremes in temperature (either too hot or too cold) will reduce the shelf life of your food. Your storage pantry should be located in a climate controlled area of your house—not in the garage or attic. The area should also be dry since moisture also reduces the shelf life of your stored food. Moisture can cause mold. It can also attract insects, mice, and other vermin.

Your storage pantry should also be dark. Exposure to sunlight will obviously raise the temperature, but prolonged exposure to any light source will reduce the effectiveness of certain vitamins and minerals. Vitamins A, E, and D are especially susceptible to breaking down when exposed to light. While the food will still be edible, you won't be getting as much nutrition from it. If you are expecting to be self-sufficient, you want your food sources to be as nutritious as possible not just to keep you from getting sick, but also to provide you with the necessary energy to perform the tasks required of you to remain safe.

While we're on the subject of safe food storage, it is also worth remembering that all stored food has an expiration date. In the event of freeze-dried food, that date could be decades in the future, but not all food will last that long. You should take an annual inventory of all of the food in your supply pantry and note the expiration dates. If you have food that is getting close to expiring, then go ahead and eat it and replace it in your pantry with new stock. Rotating food in and out like this will reduce waste since you'll be eating the nearly expired food instead of throwing away expired food. It also will prevent the unfortunate surprise of discovering spoiled food. In the event of a disaster (natural or zombie-related), you don't want to find yourself needing to dip into your supply pantry only to discover some of it has spoiled and is inedible when you don't have the option to make a quick trip to the grocery store to replace it!

Replenishing Your Food Supply

Having a stocked pantry is great, but even the best stocked pantry will run out if it is not replenished. Right now that is easy. There are no major disasters preventing you from running to the grocery store. There are no disruptions to the supply chain, so your grocery stores are well stocked. The living dead aren't walking the earth so you can get around easily. That won't always be the case, though. So what can you do to help keep your pantry stocked when a trip to the grocery store isn't so easy?

- Learn to cook the food you have—while this seems obvious, there are still many people today who rely on fast food, carryout, food delivery, and prepared food for their daily meals. Aside from being rather expensive, this isn't very practical during a disaster. If all the roads to your house are flooded, how is the pizza delivery guy going to even get to you? Also, I wouldn't count on DoorDash being available during the Zombie Apocalypse. Being able to cook will allow you to have healthy, nutritious meals that you can prepare from items you already have on-hand. You don't need to be a trained chef to make this happen, either. Take another look at the list of supplies I recommend to have in your pantry and think how many different meals you can make from them. Boil up some rice or beans with some vegetables and a little meat and you have a hearty stew for a fraction of the cost of takeout. If you have a 25 pound bag of rice or beans, you can make several meals from that. Do you have flour, water, salt, and yeast? That's all you need to make bread. Once again, homemade bread costs a fraction of what a loaf of storebought bread costs and you don't have to rely on a store for it. Bread is typically one of the first things that people "panic buy" as well so it's not unusual to find the bread aisle of your local grocery store empty after a disaster. If you can make your own food, you lessen your reliance on grocery stores and working supply chains.

- Grow your own food—I don't mean you have to start a farm, but most people have the space to grow some vegetables. Even if you don't have a lot of yard space, there are vegetable plants that are designed to grow and produce when planted in a container. Spices don't require a lot of space to grow, either. Freshly grown spices and vegetables absolutely taste better than produce purchased in a store and harvesting them from your backyard is going to be easier than trying to get to a store.
- Can your own food—did your garden do extra well and now you have a bunch of produce that you don't know what to do with? Preserve it by canning. Home canning has never been easier or safer. Granted, it's called "canning" but you are actually preserving the food in glass Mason jars—not tin cans. All you need for this is a pressure canner. A pressure canner is a large pot with a lid that locks down and a gauge on it which allows you to monitor the pressure. You pour a little water in the pot, place your sealed Mason jars of food inside, lock down the lid, and apply heat. The heat causes the water to boil and produce steam. Since the lid is locked down, the steam can't escape like it normally would, so the temperature (and pressure) inside the pot increases. The steam can reach 240 °F (116 °C) which is hot enough to kill off any microorganisms in the food which makes the canned food shelf stable. Food canned this way will remain good for about 1–2 years when properly stored. A major advantage to home canning is the variety of food you can preserve. You are not limited to just vegetables. You can also can jellies, jams, preserves, sauces, and even meat. Home canning is great for preserving extra produce grown from your garden, but don't limit yourself to just that. If you find a good sale on fresh vegetables at your grocery store, buy them, take them home, and can them. Anything you can do to replenish your supply and make yourself more self-sufficient will help.

- Dehydrate your own food—we have already established that dehydrated food is great for emergency preparedness. It is lightweight, easy to store, easy to eat, and has an unusually long shelf life. Fortunately, you are not limited to the dehydrated food you have to purchase. You can easily dehydrate your own food. Food dehydrators can be purchased online and in many retail locations (camping goods stores, "big box" stores, etc.) and quality dehydrators can be purchased for well under $100 with larger capacity units still being available for around $200. With your own food dehydrator, you can make your own jerky but you can also dehydrate many other normal household food items. Dried fruits (apples, bananas, apricots, peaches, cherries, blueberries, or pears) make for an excellent high-energy snack.

  Buy them in bulk at your grocery store when they are at the peak of their growing season (that's when the prices are the cheapest), dehydrate them and stock your pantry. Dried vegetables can be added to soups, stews, or existing meals. Carrots, mushrooms, onions, peas, beans, and tomatoes are perfect additions to help liven up what could be a bland dish. The same can be done with meat. Jerky can be eaten on its own, or dried beef, chicken, turkey, or fish can really add a lot of flavor to a meal. Nuts, seeds, and grains can be dehydrated for storage. Walnuts, hazelnuts, macadamia nuts, pecans, rice, buckwheat, barley, and quinoa are excellent for this. Fresh spices (oregano, basil, dill, fennel, mint, lemon balm, hyssop) dry perfectly for storage. Dried herbs can be used for cooking (don't feel like you have to wait for a disaster to do this—fresh herbs will always taste better than store-bought herbs) whereas delicious teas can be made from dried mint, lemon balm, ginger, thyme, lavender, and chamomile.
- Freeze-dry your own food—consumer-grade freeze dryers have become less expensive. They are still pricier than dehydrators, however. A home freeze dryer will set you back anywhere from $500 to over $2,000. The advantage, of course, is the ability to freeze dry pretty much any type of food that you have on hand. Freeze dried food retains nearly all of its nutritional content as well as its original consistency. On top of that, freeze dried food has a shelf life that is measured in decades. It remains up to your individual budget whether or not it is worth it to be able to freeze dry your own food, though. Freeze dryers are not an insignificant expense and neither are they quick. A typical freeze drying cycle can be 20 hours or more.

Not everything involving preparing for the Zombie Apocalypse has to be all doom and gloom. While survival is important, hobbies can help to lessen the stress of merely surviving from day to day. Fortunately there are some hobbies that will allow you to relax, to be creative, and to increase your food pantry in the process.

- Cheese making—many people have discovered the joy of making their own cheese. It is a great family hobby since it is inexpensive and doesn't require a lot of specialized equipment. Any kind of cheese you can find in the store can be made at home—cream cheese, ricotta, goat cheese, colby, gouda, mozzarella, cheddar. Both soft cheeses and aged hard cheeses can be made in your own home with a few simple ingredients. You just need fresh milk and rennet (plus a few other simple ingredients depending on the type of cheese you plan on making). Rennet is an enzyme that causes the milk to form into solid curds—an integral part of making cheese. And wax-sealed hard cheeses can be stored for decades.
- Home brewing—making beer or wine at home can be done with a little practice and without the need for expensive equipment. The labor part of the process doesn't take very long. A majority of the time is taken up letting the fermentation process happen. While you should avoid drinking alcohol during a disaster, there are some benefits to having it around. First and foremost, the fermentation process and the alcohol in beer and wine kills off any bacteria in the water so beer or wine is a source of uncontaminated drinking water. Before the discovery of microscopic bacteria, people had a difficult time finding a source of water to drink without making themselves sick. Beer and wine were plentiful and safer to drink than water from an unknown source. Beer and wine can also be used for barter. Maybe a neighbor has some tool or piece of equipment you need or maybe they just have some different food in their stockpile that sounds delicious. Assuming that banks are unavailable and stores are closed for business, good old fashioned trading will be how goods and services are exchanged. Homemade beer and wine are always attractive trading items.
- Hunting and fishing—granted, not everyone reading this lives in an area where hunting and fishing is practical. Obviously this is not something that you are going to be able to do if you live in a large city or densely populated metropolitan area. However, if you live in or have access to a more rural area, the ability to

hunt and fish for your own food is a valuable skill. Both are great outdoor activities. These activities can provide fresh meat for you on a regular basis. America's rivers, streams, and lakes are teeming with many different varieties of edible fish. The woods and forests are home to many types of game animals including deer, wild turkey, squirrels, grouse, elk, and wild boar.

Disaster Preparedness Kit for Your House

A stockpile of food and water and the ability to refresh your stockpile are essential, but just as in previous chapters, there are everyday items you are going to need in order to ride out the disaster. The kit for this chapter is going to have the largest number of items so far, but you are also planning on being partially or wholly self-sufficient for the longest period yet. When you can't expect UPS or Amazon to be delivering to your house nor can you rely on being able to hop in your vehicle and drive to the nearest Big Box home improvement store, you have to rely on yourself to have everything you need. While this may seem like a monumental task, you should approach as mentioned earlier—take the items for the preparedness level that you already have and simply build on them. This level of readiness is an end goal—not a starting point so don't feel like you need to go and purchase everything listed below in one trip. Take your time and be smart in your preparation. Buy things a little at a time and before you know it you will be ready to face anything from a hurricane or tornado to roving mobs of zombies.

The disaster preparedness kit for your house should include:

- A packet with a copy of all of your important documents (as detailed in Chapter 1). The packet should be inspected once a year and any out-of-date information should be corrected.
- Radios with NOAA Weather Radio—have multiple radios on hand. More radios means more than one person can be informed. More radios also means that you won't lose your single connection to the outside world in an accident. Redundancy is the key here. If two radios are good, then three would be even better. Keep different kinds, too. A larger radio with bigger speakers is perfect to fill a room with sound, but a small pocket-sized radio is just the thing to keep on your person so you can stay informed when you are outside the house. The radios should have redundant power sources, too. Electric is great, but the power is typically one of the first things that goes

out in a disaster. You can find radios today that are battery powered, solar powered, or even powered by a hand crank. Some even come with all three options. It is also not uncommon to find radios with USB charging ports so you can use the batteries, solar power, or the hand crank to charge your cell phone.

- Flashlights—just like radios, more is better. Different styles are also better. Large flashlights can provide very bright light for a long distance or light up a large room. Smaller flashlights are easy to tuck in a pocket and much more convenient to carry around.
- LED lanterns—LED lanterns are designed to light up larger areas—like a room. The LED bulbs are very bright and don't consume very much power so the batteries in them will last longer. They also remain cool to the touch when in use so there is no danger of a fire hazard like there would be with the old camping lanterns
- Batteries—radios, flashlights, and lanterns all run on batteries. You should have plenty to spare. When you think you have enough, buy another package just to be safe. Modern electronics are much more energy efficient than they used to be, but you could feasibly be using your radios and flashlights for hours on end so expect to go through batteries more quickly than in normal, non-disaster, times. Your battery supply should be completely replaced every year. The printed shelf life of the batteries is much longer than a year, but it is better to err on the side of caution. These devices are going to be your lifelines and it is extremely important that they work when you need them to.
- First aid kit—again, you are going to want to have multiple kits in different places. The ability to administer quality first aid could be the difference between life and death or at the very least between sickness, pain, and health. This is another area where a pre-packaged first aid kit is probably not going to suffice for your needs. I would recommend building your own. It should include:
    - ◊ A sturdy case—you are going to be collecting a bunch of different items for your first aid kit and you're obviously going to need somewhere to store them all. I would recommend a duffel bag or backpack and preferably one that is water resistant and made of a brightly colored fabric. You want your case to be tough enough to stand up to the knocking around you are going to put it through. A brightly colored case will make it easy to find.

◊ 1 pair of tweezers—for removing splinters and other foreign objects. Try not to buy the cheapest pair you can find since you're planning on not being able to run out to the drugstore at a moment's notice if the ones you have break.

◊ Thermometer—a non-contact thermal thermometer will serve you better than a traditional mercury-filled glass thermometer if for no other reason than a non-contact thermometer will provide you with a temperature reading quicker. You might be trying to take the temperature of someone who is agitated—the Zombie Virus will do that to people. At the very least, just imagine how difficult it is to get a small child to sit still and hold a traditional thermometer under their tongue long enough for it to get an accurate reading. A quick reading is always better.

◊ Cotton swabs—perfect for cleaning wounds. They are available in bulk and some brands even sell them treated with an antibacterial solution for extra protection.

◊ Trauma shears—also known as medical scissors or EMT shears, these are not your standard scissors. Trauma shears are designed with sharp, serrated edges treated with a non-stick coating which gives them the ability to quickly and cleanly cut through tough material (bandages, several layers of clothing, etc.). Trauma shears also have a blunt tip so they can be slid along someone's skin (while in the process of cutting off restrictive clothing, for example) without cutting them.

◊ Surgical-grade toenail clippers—Sure, a hangnail seems like a minor inconvenience during the Zombie Apocalypse, but minor issues like this can develop into serious issues if left untreated. I recommend toenail clippers instead of fingernail clippers for the simple reason that toenail clippers are bigger and stronger. They can be used for more than just clipping fingernails, too. They are perfect for cutting away zip ties, for example.

◊ Scalpel—for the purpose of your first aid kit, I would recommend a box of disposable scalpels. They are cheap and easy to store and you never have to worry about them being sharp or sterile when you need to use them.

◊ Stethoscope—obviously used for listening for heartbeats, stethoscopes can also be used to listen to someone's breathing to check for congestion in the lungs.

◊ Suture kit—some cuts are just too big to seal back up on

their own and will require stitches or sutures. For this purpose, a pre-packaged suture kit will suffice, Most suture kits will include needles, nylon sutures, a suture driver (or needle holder—used to hold the needle during the suturing process), and a series of hemostats (or medical clamps). Some higher-end suture kits will even come with patches of synthetic skin to practice suturing on.

◊ Blister treatment—sold under names like Molefoam, Moleskin or 2nd Skin, these products will help prevent blisters from forming. Even a generous application of medical tape in a blister-prone area will help. Blisters are caused by friction and pressure so anything you can do to lessen either factor will help. Padding around an existing blister will prevent it from getting larger. A blister that breaks open, aside from being painful, can lead to infection since a broken blister is essentially an open wound.
◊ Irrigation syringe—helpful in cleaning out a wound to get it ready for treatment.
◊ Absorbent compress dressings (5" × 9")—Typically these are sold in a box of 25 dressings. I would recommend at least one box or two if you have the room in your kit.
◊ Adhesive bandages (assorted sizes)—As many boxes as you have room for, but no less than 50 bandages total of different sizes.
◊ Sterile gauze pads—Most commonly sold in 4" × 4" size in boxes of 100. At least one box should be in your kit.
◊ Antiseptic wipes—at least one 50-count box
◊ Emergency blanket—also known as space blankets, mylar blankets, or first aid blankets, these are very light weight, very reflective, plastic sheets and are excellent at keeping you warm. They are designed to trap up to 90 percent of the heat generated by the body and prevent it from being lost to the air by convection. The bottom line—these are cheap, don't take up much space, and an invaluable addition to your first aid kit. Have multiples for everyone you expect to be sheltering with you.
◊ Ace bandages—for wrapping sprains or supporting sore joints. You should have at least two rolls.
◊ Triangle bandages—these can be used as large dressings, to secure a dressing in place, or as an arm sling. You should have at least two.
◊ Tegaderm bandages—these are transparent dressings used

to provide a moist environment for wound healing, Typically they are used for minor burns or abrasions—anywhere that you want to cover a wound and prevent more damage from friction. I recommend one box of eight bandages.

◊ Butterfly bandages—Also known as "steri-strips," these are used as an alternative to conventional sutures. They can be used to help close larger wounds, uneven wounds, or even wounds that are bleeding heavily. They are also very handy to close wounds in areas that are difficult to bandage—areas that are moist or move frequently. If you have an injury that you would typically go to the ER for stitches for, but circumstances prevent you from going, treating the injury with butterfly bandages is a very effective wound treatment.

◊ SAM splint—a SAM (structural aluminum malleable) splint is a modern answer to a traditional splint when immobilizing a body part. A SAM splint is essentially a thin strip of aluminum covered by closed-cell foam. They are generally found in either folded flat strips or on a roll. The splint is unfolded or unrolled, then formed around the body part (a wrist, shin, or forearm for example). Once the SAM splint is shaped into a curve, it becomes quite rigid thus providing the stability to prevent further injury. These splints can also be cut down to a smaller size to splint fingers. They also have the added advantage of being reusable—simply clean it off and reroll it and it is ready to be used again. You should have at least two SAM splints.

◊ Israeli bandage—Also known as an Emergency Bandage, combines an elastic bandage, a sterile non-adherent dressing, and a device to provide direct pressure to the wound. Israeli bandages have proven vital in the treatment of hemorrhagic wounds (wounds with heavy bleeding) and are a staple item in any first aid kit and you should have at least one.

◊ Tourniquet—another potential life-saving device used to stop bleeding. You should have at least one in your kit.

◊ Chest seal—Originally used by combat medics, chest seals have worked their way down to where they are available for civilians to use. The chest seal itself is a pretty straightforward design. It is a dressing about 6" in size that has one side covered in a very strong adhesive. Chest seals can be either vented or unvented. This premise is very simple: any deep puncture wound on the upper torso has the potential to puncture a person's lung. When that happens, the dreaded "sucking chest wound" occurs where air starts to escape from a person's lung and begins to fill the space between their lung and their chest wall. This buildup of air then begins to put pressure on the lung so it is no longer able to expand and fill up. This results in a condition called pneumothorax or more commonly known as a collapsed lung.

A chest seal works by making an airtight seal to prevent any more air from entering the chest cavity. Vented chest seals have a one-way vent built into them to allow air to escape whereas the unvented ones just seal the wound. The common thinking is to apply a chest seal to a person if they have a wound on their upper torso that may have punctured their lung—whether or not they are experiencing any symptoms (shortness of breath, etc.). Medically you won't harm anyone by applying a chest seal even if they don't have a punctured lung. Although speaking as someone who has had several of these applied to me as part of a training exercise, they hurt to take off. The adhesive on them is designed to stick to skin regardless of blood, sweat, or other bodily fluids so the adhesive is VERY strong. I recommend one chest seal to be in your kit. Vented or unvented is not that important although unvented are less expensive.

◊ 1 box of nonlatex gloves
◊ 1 instant cold compress
◊ Clotting agents—sold under the brand names of QuickClot and Celox, clotting agents contain an ingredient that promotes rapid blood clotting. The quicker a bleeding wound clots, the quicker the bleeding stops. Original clotting agents were sold as a granular power that was literally poured directly into the wound area. Newer ones have the clotting agent impregnated into a gauze bandage which is applied directly to the bleeding area.
◊ 1 permanent marker—there are countless reasons for needing to write something down in an emergency. If you ever need to apply a tourniquet, you should write on the tourniquet the time that it was applied in order to prevent its being left on too long, for example.
◊ Small flashlight—a light shone directly in the eye will cause the pupil to react. The quickness of the reaction (or

lack of reaction) can be used to indicate a brain injury or impairment. A flashlight is handy for more obvious reasons, too—you can't always count on there being sufficient light to see what you're doing when you are trying to administer aid to someone.
    - ◊ First aid guide—all of the equipment in the world will not be helpful to you if you don't know how to use it or how to use it correctly. Seconds count when administering first aid, but don't cause further harm by administering incorrect techniques. You should be comfortable with first aid techniques before attempting them—especially techniques involving treatment of more serious injuries.
    - ◊ Clearly label everything—Know the items in your kit and label anything that does not have an obvious label designating exactly what it is. In an emergency, the last thing you want to do is to rummage around in your First Aid Kit looking for a specific item and trying to differentiate one unmarked package from another.
- 30 day supply of prescription medication—we are assuming that you are not going to be able to pop out to the pharmacy for a refill and that delivery services will be interrupted for a protracted period of time so a refill by mail will not be a viable option. You should have at minimum a 30 day supply of all prescription medication that you and anyone sheltering with you will need. Don't forget about your pets. If they take any prescription medication, be sure to have a supply of that on hand as well. Personally, I would consider a 30 day supply to be the bare minimum if you are expecting to be self-sufficient for four weeks. A 60 to 90 day supply would be a much better idea, provided that is feasible.
- Over-the-counter (OTC) drugs—while a well-stocked first aid kit and a supply of necessary prescription medication will go a long way, not every issue you encounter is going to need this level of treatment. There are many excellent treatment options available for purchase without a prescription. You should stock:
    - ◊ Aspirin—pain reliever, fever reducer, blood thinner. Aspirin would be an essential item just for that, but it can also be great to reduce muscle aches, headaches, toothaches, and even help someone recover from a heart attack or to prevent future ones. Stock at least one large bottle.
    - ◊ Ibuprofen—Ibuprofen serves to both relieve pain and reduce

inflammation and swelling. It can also reduce fever. Stock at least one large bottle.

- ◊ Antacids—Stress can wreak havoc on your digestive system. Ulcers can form or be made worse for those who already have them. Stock at least one bottle.
- ◊ Antihistamines—No power means no air conditioner which means more open windows and more time outside. Anyone with seasonal allergies will know the misery of a flare up. Antihistamines will help quell the symptoms of common allergic reactions including runny nose, sneezing, watery eyes, hives, conjunctivitis (pink eye), and the itching and swelling that accompany insect bites. Stock one large bottle—or more if you are particularly prone to allergies.
- ◊ Bismuth subsalicylate—Pink bismuth (more commonly sold as Pepto-Bismol) is an effective treatment for indigestion, nausea, heartburn, gas, and diarrhea. Most of those symptoms will just make you feel bad, but diarrhea can be dangerous and even deadly when left untreated. Aside from the obvious digestive issues, you will quickly become dehydrated due to the extra loss of fluids. Dehydration in a disaster situation is nothing to take lightly. Stock one bottle or box of tablets (depending on your preference).
- ◊ Cough medicine—There are two major categories of cough medicine: antitussives are cough suppressants (they block the body's cough reflex) whereas expectorants thin the mucus and make it easier to clear when you cough. Both have their purposes. Someone who is sick and coughing can spread their sickness. On the other hand, being congested and unable to cough the mucus free from your lungs can lead to many dangerous conditions—including pneumonia. Stock one bottle of your preferred brand.
- ◊ Pseudoephedrine—sold under many different brand names, pseudoephedrine acts to treat the symptoms of seasonal allergies, but it also treats the symptoms of the common cold and sinusitis (stuffy nose and sinus pain and pressure). Stock enough to provide you with enough doses to last 30 days.
- ◊ Throat lozenges—throat lozenges are another way of soothing a cough or treating an irritated throat which can be caused by colds or allergies. Medicated lozenges have an anesthetic as a pain reducer. Stock one bag.
- ◊ Oral rehydration—essentially water with a small amount of

sugar, sodium, and potassium. Oral rehydration products are consumed to prevent or treat dehydration. These are sold in ready-to-drink bottles in various brand names—with the brand Pedialyte being one of the best known. There are also many manufacturers who produce oral rehydration products as powder which is dissolved in water and consumed that way. I recommend one box of the powered products since they are much easier to store.

◊ Laxatives—Just like diarrhea can kill, constipation can also kill if left untreated. Stress coupled with foods that might be outside of your normal diet can lead to digestive distress. Stock one box of laxatives and/or stool softener.

◊ Sleep aids—The stress of a disaster can make it difficult to sleep. Not getting enough sleep will leave a person groggy and "brain fogged" and so unable to make quick decisions or act with good judgment. This can be dangerous or even deadly in the wake of a natural disaster. Stock one package.

◊ Cranberry extract—sold in bottles or in capsule form, cranberry extract is full of antioxidants which have many health benefits. The main reason for the inclusion on this list is the fact that cranberry extract helps prevent urinary tract infections (UTIs). Aside from being painful, the infection from an untreated UTI may spread to the bladder and kidneys. If your circumstances prevent you from seeking medical help potentially for weeks, coming down with a UTI could be very serious. If you or anyone you are sheltering with has a problem with reoccurring UTIs, stock at least one bottle of Cranberry extract capsules.

◊ Saline spray—sold as a decongestant, saline solution can also be used to help irrigate wounds, flush debris from eyes, and even clean your contact lenses. This is on top of the fact that saline solution also helps moisten dry nasal passages and curbs inflammation of mucous membranes. Stock two or three bottles.

◊ Vitamins—Despite your best efforts, the food you eat to survive probably won't have the necessary amount of vitamins that you would normally get otherwise. Even a basic multivitamin will help ensure you stay as healthy as you can until the disaster is over. It goes without saying that your overall health is paramount to your survival. Stock one large bottle of a traditional multivitamin.

◊ Antibiotic ointment—perfect for treating minor wounds or

skin infections, antibiotic ointment also helps prevent these minor wounds from becoming infected. Stock two tubes.
    - ◊ Hydrocortisone cream—used to treat insect bites, poison oak, poison ivy, eczema, dermatitis, rashes, and itchy skin. Stock one tube.
    - ◊ Miconazole cream—used to treat skin conditions that are fungal in nature like athlete's foot, jock itch, or even ringworm. Stock one tube.
    - ◊ Antibacterial soap—used in cleaning wounds. The added antibacterial properties will help to get the wound cleaner and make it less prone to infection. Stock one bar.
- Signal mirror or whistle—when you need to get someone's attention, using a signal mirror or loud whistle is much more effective than just yelling. After a large-scale disaster, emergency personnel will generally make their way through the area to assess the damage and to check on the wellbeing of anyone in the area. A signal mirror or whistle is an excellent way to get their attention and make your presence known. A flash of light reflected from a signal mirror can be seen for several miles under the right conditions. Emergency whistles are quite loud—with some approaching 125 decibels. A whistle that loud can easily be heard up to half a mile away. To fully prepare for all circumstances, have both a signal mirror AND a signal whistle. A signal mirror will not be much use to you in the dark or on a cloudy day. A signal whistle, as loud as they are, can be drowned out by louder sounds.
- Lumber—keep on hand several 4' × 8' sheets of plywood plus as many smaller boards as you can comfortably store. Strong winds can damage roofs and other structures. Strong enough winds can blow large items around and can break windows and doors. Keeping your home safe and secure will involve repairing that damage as best as you can. Patch any holes in your roof or walls and board up any broken windows or damaged doors. Should certain parts of your house be too damaged to provide protection from the elements, the same lumber can be used to block those areas of your house off. You ultimately want the area you are sheltering in to be closed off from the outside world. Any open spaces will let in wind, rain, snow as well as any animals or vermin. Rain or snow will cause more damage to your structure. Areas where the wind can get in will make it difficult to heat. Animals or vermin getting into your house could expose you to disease if you are bitten or the animals

could get into your food supply corrupting it so it is not usable for you and your family.

- Hammer and nails—having all the lumber in the world is not going to help you board up a broken window if you don't have any way to secure it. Power tools (even cordless ones) are great, but we are assuming that you are sheltering without power. Cordless power tools still take a battery which will need to be recharged. Having a manual solution to this is always a good backup.
- Tarps or plastic sheets—tarps can be used as a substitute for wood when patching up your structure. A tarp can serve as a makeshift fix for a damaged roof or can quickly and easily block off a damaged door or broken window. They serve more purposes than that, though. A tarp can serve as an emergency blanket in a pinch or DIY rain wear. A tarp can be spread out on wet ground to provide you a dry place to sit or lie down. A tarp can be used to help move debris—pile the debris on the tarp and drag it away. In a pinch, a tarp and some paint can be used to make a quick sign. All in all, tarps are very versatile items. They can be purchased in many different sizes—from small enough to be used as a rain poncho to large enough to cover your entire roof. They also come in different thicknesses for different applications. Buy several in various sizes. Plastic sheets are just as versatile as tarps, but generally made of a thinner material. I wouldn't recommend patching a roof with a plastic sheet, but they can definitely be used to help seal off a window or room. The easiest way to get plastic sheets is to look for drop cloths in the painting section of your local Big Box hardware store. They can be purchased very inexpensively and, due to their intended use, are quite large.
- Duct tape—easily the most versatile item on this list, the roll of duct tape is an absolute essential. If you encounter a problem, there's a good chance that you can fix it (at least partially) with duct tape. Use it to patch broken windows or hold damaged doors closed. If you need to seal off an area, plastic sheets and duct tape will make an airtight seal. Have a bucket or bottle with a crack or hole it in? Patch it with duct tape. Use duct tape as an improvised bandage or sling. While you're at it, duct tape is perfect for quickly patching a hole in your shoe or a tear in your clothing. Weave strips of duct tape together and you've made a strong cord. Need to mark an area or leave a sign? Duct tape and a permanent marker make for a very effective sign. You can even

take this a step further by fashioning directional arrows out of duct tape to help clarify your message. Also don't forget the obvious use of using duct tape to attach something to something else. Duct tape is available in different thicknesses, colors, and sizes. My personal recommendation is to get as much as you can reasonably store.

- Plastic zip ties—these are right up there with duct tape on the usefulness and versatility scale. They work just as well as duct tape in many situations that involve attaching something to something else. They are perfect for on-the-go repairs and tying items down, but their non-adhesiveness gives them some unique applications. Naturally you're going to want to pack the items in your home preparedness kit as efficiently as possible to maximize the available space. If you are packing clothing, fold the clothes and place them in a zip-lock bag. Squeeze all of the air out of the bag and then roll it up as tightly as possible. Secure the rolled up item with zip ties. When the time comes to use the clothes, just clip the zip ties away. Not only does this technique save space, but it also helps keep your clothes dry.

  On the subject of clothes, zip ties can make great gaiters—just tuck the hem of your pants into your socks, blouse the pants over a little bit and zip tie them snugly to your leg. This is perfect for when you need to walk through tall grass in an area where ticks abound. Having the hem of your pants sealed off prevents ticks and the like from crawling up under your clothing where you won't notice them. Similarly, you can wrap several loops of zip ties around your shoes to give you extra traction when you're walking in snow and ice. Since they are designed to close tightly and not come loose, zip ties make a great makeshift tourniquet. If you have an area that you need to keep secure, secure a door closed with zip ties. Aside from keeping the door closed, this also allows you to know if the area has remained secure since nobody can enter the door without cutting the zip tie. Zip ties come in many shapes, sizes, colors, and strengths. Just like duct tape, stock up as much as you can conveniently store.
- Face covering—if you recall the Survivability Rule of 3, breathable air is the single most important component. You only have about 3 minutes to live in an area with no breathable air. Natural disasters can make the air hazardous in many ways. The air could be filled with smoke, dust, fumes, or other particulate matter that makes it dangerous to breathe. Your emergency kit should have a good supply of face coverings. Previous chapters

provided a detailed explanation on the different types of face coverings. For the purpose of protection in this scenario, I would recommend having at least one box of N95 respirator masks for yourself and anyone you plan on sheltering with you. An N95 respirator mask should provide you with adequate protection for most situations. Awareness of your situation will help you decide if you need more robust protection in the form of cartridge-based respirator masks. If you live near railroad tracks or major highways where potentially hazardous material is regularly transported, then the added protection of a cartridge-based respirator mask could be a good option to have on hand. These respirator masks can provide protection against chemical agents and so could give you additional protection in the case of an accident or train derailment that causes a chemical spill.

A cartridge-based respirator mask might also be a worthy addition if you live downwind from a business that processes or handles hazardous chemicals. A surefire way to know if you do is to simply take a drive around your immediate area. It may not be obvious what a particular company does by their name, so be on the lookout for a windsock on the property like you would normally see at airports. If you see a business that has one of those orange windsocks on their property, you can likely assume they don't have it there for decoration! Any business that has something on their property that shows them the direction that the wind is blowing most likely has that in place because they have something on their property that could be hazardous if it escaped into the air. The windsocks are in place so they know the speed and direction that the prevailing winds will blow any noxious gasses. If your house happens to be downwind from one of these companies, you should keep that in mind when planning for your safety.

- Moist towelettes—Just like comfort food goes a long way to keeping you feeling "normal" during a disaster, so does keeping clean. In a situation where you have no access to running water (or at the very least no access to hot water), moist towelettes are a very effective way to keep clean and sanitary. Don't be fooled by the "towelette" name, either—these are not the little things you get in restaurants after you've had a serving of wings. Some brands of towelettes are the size of washcloths and so can absolutely serve as a replacement for a shower. Even if you do have access to water, a supply of moist towelettes used for personal sanitation will prevent you from having to use your drinking water supply for cleaning and so will help make your water last longer. These typically come in resealable packages and store very easily. Cleanliness is important so be sure to have several packages on hand.

- Feminine hygiene products. No emergency kit would be complete without a supply of the necessary products for each woman in your household. They have more than their intended uses as well. There have been several documented cases of U.S. Army medics using tampons as improvised bandages. They are sterile, designed to be ultra-absorbent, and individually packaged in waterproof pouches. While not a real substitute for a bandage, they can certainly be used as a stopgap measure until more formal first aid can be administered. You should keep at least one month's supply of all necessary items for each woman you expect to be sheltering with you.
- Garbage bags—common garbage bags can serve many purposes in a disaster situation.
  - ◊ Refuse disposal—of course you can use garbage bags for their intended purpose. Bag up any trash you want removed from your area. Keep in mind, if the disaster is bad enough your normal trash pickup service will likely be interrupted so be mindful of where you store bagged trash. Piles of refuse can attract vermin and animals.
  - ◊ Waterproof storage—garbage bags are waterproof and so they make a quick and convenient way to store anything that you want to keep dry.
  - ◊ Improvised tarp—cut garbage bags open to create a smaller tarp or larger plastic sheet to provide waterproof coverage for items stored outside.
  - ◊ Rain poncho—if you're caught out without rain gear, a garbage bag can provide you with an effective improvised rain poncho.
  - ◊ Ground cover—spread out on the ground, a garbage bag can provide a clean, dry place to put something down—even yourself.
  - ◊ Water heater—Partially fill a dark colored garbage bag with water and place it in direct sunlight. This will warm up the water inside. This process can also be used to melt snow into drinkable water.
  - ◊ Shower—use the above technique to make warm water, then hang the bag from a tree and poke some holes in the bottom to create a makeshift shower.

- ◊ Shoe/hand protectors—put garbage bags on your feet, run the bags as far up your legs as necessary and secure them with duct tape. This will allow you to walk through deep water or mud while keeping your feet clean and dry. Use a similar technique on your hands and arms when you need to handle anything that you'd prefer to not have on your hands.
- ◊ First aid—Garbage bags can be cut into strips to be used as ties to secure bandages. Several can be formed into a sling. Garbage bags cut into larger shapes can be used to provide a waterproof cover for wounds or to make a waterproof cast.
- ◊ Bedding—fill garbage bags with leaves or moss to create a functional pillow (or mattress if you use enough).
- ◊ Makeshift toilet—Garbage bags and a 5-gallon bucket can be used to make a toilet. Doing this will also help you extend your water supply since you won't need to use drinkable water to flush your toilet. The idea behind this works pretty much as you'd expect—line the bucket with a garbage bag, conduct your business, then remove the bag, tie it closed and dispose of it. Sprinkle sawdust or kitty litter in the bag between uses. I recommend stocking a couple of boxes of garbage bags. You should preferably use the "contractor style" bags instead of regular garbage bags since the contractor bags are typically larger and thicker than regular garbage bags and so more durable.

- Utility shut-off tool—if you need a special tool to shut off any of your utilities, you should keep that tool in your emergency supply kit. Depending on the type of disaster, you might need to quickly turn off your utilities in order to prevent further damage. Any widespread electrical issues in your house would require you to turn off the power to your house at the main circuit breaker. A gas leak would necessitate immediately shutting off the gas supply to your house at the main supply shutoff. A specialized utility shut-off tool is also going to be made of a non-sparking alloy for obvious reasons. If you are shutting off a leaking gas line, the last thing you want is a stray spark.
- Multi-tool—despite the fact that you are sheltering in your house, it is still a good idea to have a multi-tool in your Emergency Preparation Kit. You'll have access to all of the tools in your house, but in a disaster you will need quick access to them. When seconds count, you don't need to be rummaging around in your garage or your "junk drawer" to find a screwdriver or a pair of pliers.

- Manual can opener—the best stocked pantry of canned food is of no use if the power goes out and you can't open the cans. Don't feel like you're limited to the traditional hand-cranked can opener, either. First developed by the U.S. military in 1942, the classic P-38 can opener is small enough to be attached to a keychain and durable enough to last for years. The P-38 is also inexpensive enough that you can (and should) have several around. Don't overlook the P-38's big brother—the P-51 can opener. The P-51 was designed to open larger cans, but many people have found its slightly larger size makes it easier to use on standard cans. The U.S. military doesn't have the market cornered in the can opener area, either. The Australian Defense Force and New Zealand Army both use a device known as the FRED (field ration eating device) which is a slightly larger style of the P-51 with a small spoon and bottle opener built into it.
- Battery packs—you should have at least one quality battery pack for each cellphone in your house. Make sure the battery pack has the correct cable to charge your phone as well. High quality battery packs are available now at very reasonable prices and can have the capacity to fully charge your cell phone multiple times. Sparing use of your cellphone will naturally help extend the battery life. Keep in mind that battery packs will act as a "trickle charger" so it will take several hours to completely charge your phone from a dead battery and you should have your phone powered off while charging to further help extend its battery life.
- Blankets—it doesn't take long for a house to cool off when the heat goes out—even on a relatively moderate day. Keep a blanket or two per person in a handy location that you can grab quickly. Having more blankets available is also a good idea, but those can be stored away for retrieval later.
- Sleeping bags—You're going to be sheltering in your house so you are more than likely going to be able to sleep in your own bed. A sleeping bag is still a very handy thing to have. Sleeping in a sleeping bag in your bed will provide you with some added warmth on a cold night with no heat. They can be useful when it is hot as well. On hot nights without access to an air conditioner, sometimes the best way to keep cool is to sleep outside. Even on the hottest nights, it can still get cool enough that some type of cover would be helpful. One thing to keep in mind when shopping for a sleeping bag is that not all sleeping bags are created equal. The overall weight of the sleeping bag and the

type of insulation it uses are two major points to consider—although not so much for this scenario. Equipment weight is vital to consider for backpackers since they (by nature of the activity) have to carry all of their gear. When looking to use a sleeping bag to help you shelter in place, the weight of the bag is not all that important. The same can be said for the type of material used to fill and insulate the bag.

The choices are a synthetic fill or a natural fill with the natural filling typically being down feathers. Down-filled sleeping bags are much lighter and dry out quicker when they get wet, but they are significantly more expensive. For this type of sheltering situation, a sleeping bag with a synthetic filling will more than suffice. The only choice that remains is the sleeping bag's temperature rating. The temperature rating of a sleeping bag is the lowest temperature at which you can use the sleeping bag and be kept comfortable. Lightweight or what are considered "summer bags" are rated at 35 degrees and up—meaning that you will stay comfortable in this type of bag as long as the temperature doesn't get below 35 degrees. More robust sleeping bags are rated between 15 degrees and 30 degrees with dedicated "winter bags" rated to 10 degrees or even lower. In all likelihood, you won't need a sleeping bag rated for extremely low temperatures for sheltering in your house. A lightweight summer bag should more than suffice and would also be the least expensive option.

- One complete change of clothes (weather appropriate)—regardless of what form the disaster takes, it will most likely come as a surprise to you—or at the very least it will happen very quickly. As a result, you could be caught outside when a strong storm moves through and completely soaked by a downpour or jolted out of bed by the sound of tornado sirens going off. At best, you're going to be uncomfortable. At worst, this could be dangerous. Wearing wet clothes in cold weather, for example, can quickly result in hypothermia.
- Rain poncho, boots, and gloves—at some point you will need to go outside to check your house for damage and make repairs. You will want to do this as quickly as possible after the event to avoid the situation getting any worse. Windborne debris can break a window and if the window isn't repaired (or at least covered), then any further rain, snow, or debris will be blown into your house. A rain poncho will keep you dry while you are out in the elements. A good pair of boots will protect your feet

since there will most likely be debris on the ground that you don't want to step on. A pair of work gloves will protect your hands from injury.

- Notepad and pen—these can come in handy for several reasons. Sure, you can use them to take notes of important information, but you can also create labels, signs for doors or windows, or write down critical information for someone else. There are special notebooks that allow you to write on them even when they are wet. These are handy, but not essential. The primary thing is to have something to write on and something to write with. For the latter, I recommend either a pencil or a permanent marker since normal pens can leak, break, or just not write on certain surfaces. A pencil or permanent marker will allow you to be able to write on pretty much anything.
- Paper map of the local area—sure, you know your way around your neighborhood and you've got the GPS on your phone for everything else. Well, suppose you can't rely on either. Phones can be damaged or their batteries can run down. Heavy cloud cover can prevent the GPS from getting a good signal. Besides, you are better off using your phone's limited battery life for something else other than navigation. Furthermore, it's one thing to know your way around your local area from the road, but a natural disaster can make roads impassible and bridges unsafe. Walking through an area looks very different than driving and an area in the wake of a natural disaster can be almost unrecognizable—landmarks can be destroyed, street signs can be down. Having a paper map (and the ability to navigate with it) can come in very handy.
- Cash—If the power goes out or can't be relied on to stay up, some businesses will still operate. Without power they will not be able to process credit card transactions—keep in mind that this will likely be the case with a prolonged Internet outage since many credit card processors rely on an Internet connection in order to verify the transactions. Any business remaining open during this will be operating on a "cash only" basis. It also stands to reason that a widespread power outage will prevent ATMs from working as well. Not knowing how long it will be before reliable power returns, you should have about $250 in small denomination bills stored away.
- Paper plates and plastic utensils—using disposable plates and utensils will prevent you from having to dip into your water supply to do your dishes. Have your meals and then just throw

the plates away. The less water you use for extraneous purposes, the longer your drinkable water supply will last—and when your drinkable water has to be purified before use, you want to make the supply last as long as you can.

- Books, magazines, board games—No power means no television and no computers. You may still have your phone, but you shouldn't be using its limited battery life for watching videos or playing games when you might need it later for something more urgent. We all spend a lot of time watching or using some type of electronic device and with the power out, you will need to find something to occupy that time. Granted, you are going to be rather busy for a while making sure everyone is safe and your shelter is secure, but once you settle into your new daily routine, you'll be surprised at how much spare time you'll have to fill. Books, magazines, board games, even storytelling will all help you pass the time. If you have children sheltering with you, having something to help keep them occupied becomes even more important. Family reading time or family board game nights are not just great ways to help pass the time, but they can also calm nerves in what can be very stressful situations. Doing something that provides a sense of normalcy is very important in situations with a lot of uncertainty. Doing "normal things" will help restore a sense of calm and will help you remind everyone that this situation—regardless of how uncertain and upsetting it is—will pass and life will return to what it was before the disaster struck.
- Pet supplies—as stressful and unpredictable as a natural disaster is on you, it can be even more stressful and unpredictable for your pets. They will have no idea what is going on and they will be thrust into a situation where they will be exposed to unusual situations, loud noises, and other unwelcome interruptions to their normal routine. Keep in mind that just having you around will bring them comfort and a sense of normalcy which will help reduce their stress. Frankly, spending this time with them will also be a stress relief for you, too. There have been many studies that have shown that interacting with your pets during times of stress has a calming effect on pet owners.
    - ◊ Food and water—naturally when you are stocking your pantry with food and water, you should make sure that your supplies include enough for your pets as well.
    - ◊ Medication—should your pet require any medication, you should have at least 30 days' worth on hand. Keep in

mind this also extends to any heartworm or flea and tick medication they need.

◊ Shelter—if you have a crate-trained dog, then they should shelter in their crate. The crate should be large enough for the animal to stand up and turn around in. Fill the crate with blankets or other warm bedding material. If your pet doesn't do well in crates, then have an area to make them as comfortable as possible. Extra blankets on the couch next to you can be an excellent place for them to feel safe.

◊ Treats and toys—yummy treats and fun toys will help to both occupy their time and keep them from getting bored. They will also provide them with a sense of normalcy and help relax them in a stressful event.

◊ Extra leash and collar—be sure to stock an extra leash and collar (or harness). The collar should have an ID tag with your name and contact information, rabies vaccination information, and any local dog tags required by your community. You don't know when a disaster will strike or what the circumstances will be and so you will need a way to make sure your pet stays safe. Some animals react to loud noises by running and hiding and the last thing you want to have happen is for your pet to get frightened and run out of your house. With all of the pertinent information on your pet's collar this will both demonstrate that your pet has an owner and is not just a stray running around as well as provide the necessary information to help reunite you with your pet.

◊ First aid kit—while similar to a first aid kit for humans, I would still recommend having one specially set aside for your pet. It should include:

One roll of cotton bandage
One roll of bandage tape
Scissors
Antibiotic ointment
Non latex gloves
Saline solution
Isopropyl alcohol
Pet first aid guide

Generators

Seeing as how you are preparing for being self-sufficient for weeks at a time, generators before more popular options. A good generator will allow you to have power to at least some important appliances in your house (your refrigerator, for example) as long as you have the ability to keep the generator fueled and running. Generators come in two types: portable and standby.

Portable Generators

Portable generators are smaller gasoline-powered generators. These can be purchased from most hardware stores and they can range in price from about $500 to $1,500. Portable generators are convenient in that they can easily be moved into place when needed and stored away when they are not. Portable generators are designed to power devices that are plugged directly into them and they typically only have the capacity to run one or two appliances. You will most likely be able to provide power to your refrigerator and maybe a lamp or two. You will not have enough capacity to run your furnace or air conditioner, though, so you will have to pick and choose what is most important. Portable generators are also relatively small so they have a smaller gas tank on them. Naturally, you will need to be able to come up with enough gasoline to keep your generator running.

Standby Generators

Standby generators are larger generators that can power your entire house. They are also typically fueled by either natural gas or propane and some can even be installed so they connect to the natural gas line coming into your house. The downside to standby generators is that they can be very expensive—ranging in price from $5,000 to easily over $20,000. These also need to be professionally installed, so there is a substantial up-front cost involved with that, too. If you happen to live in an area where the power is unstable or can be out for long periods of time, a standby generator can be a worthwhile investment. They can certainly make remaining self-sufficient during a prolonged power outage much easier.

Day-to-Day Life After the Zombie Apocalypse

By this point you will have established a safe, secure shelter that is protected from the elements. Any damage done to it will have been repaired—even if the repairs are makeshift. You will have accounted for the safety of all of your family members and you know the status and whereabouts of any family members who are not present in your house with you. You are secure in the fact that you have enough food and water for you and everyone with you (pets included) to last several weeks and you are prepared to hunker down for the long haul until the roving bands of undead are finally dealt with or until the natural disaster has passed and services are restored to you.

In *The Walking Dead,* Rick and the group of survivors got a small taste of this on Hershel's farm when they took refuge in the prison. They saw this on a larger scale when they encountered the communities of Alexandrea and the Hilltop Colony. These were established communities which had reached the point where they began to attempt to restore some type of "normal" life even during the Zombie Apocalypse. At some point, your situation will be the same. Once you are out of "survival mode" it is time to settle back in to your normal routine—or at least as normal a routine as you can. You will obviously need to be able to prepare food and clean up afterwards. At some point you will probably have to return to your job, so all the normal routines of showering, washing clothes, and the like will have to continue. So how does that look?

Food Preparation and Cleanup

This is probably the easiest item to prepare for. If you are reading this, then you already have several weeks' worth of non-perishable food stockpiled in your pantry, with the ability to replenish your supplies through barter or other methods we have previously discussed. While most non-perishable food can be eaten cold, it certainly is more appetizing when it is warmed up—plus a warm meal goes a long way to creating a feeling of security and normalcy. Your everyday backyard grill or camp stove makes an excellent way to heat up your food. With drinkable water potentially in short supply, you will want to minimize the need for using your stockpiled water supply for mundane tasks like washing dishes. If you have access to running water (such as a river, creek, or stream) you can use that source to clean up your dishes after eating. If you don't have access to running water, then using disposable plates and utensils go a long way to helping you save your water supply. Having your meals on disposable plates means you can simply throw them away (or bury or burn them) after eating and not have to worry about using your limited supply of drinkable water to wash dishes.

Personal Hygiene

Showering

You're still going to want to go out into society and so you're going to have to take reasonable measures to keep yourself presentable.

More importantly than that, keeping yourself clean will help keep you healthy as it will prevent the spread of parasites and diseases brought on by exposure to dirt. This is still possible with no running water and no power (and so no running hot water), but it does take a little more preparation.

Earlier in this chapter, I mentioned how you could create a makeshift shower with a garbage bag. While not a great long-term solution, this is still a very feasible method. To accomplish this, all you need are a few black garbage bags, some rope, and a few tree branches.

- Double-bag some black garbage bags and fill them with a few gallons of water. Water is quite heavy so experiment with the correct amount of water in the bags. You want enough water to provide you with a shower, but not so much that the bags won't support the weight.
- Once you have the correct amount of water in the bags, hang them in a place where they will get the most exposure to the sun. It makes the most sense to do this early in the morning so that bags can be in the sun for the longest amount of time. The black bags will soak up the sun and heat the water inside them to a very comfortable temperature.
- Cut four green branches to about 2.5' in length and fasten them together at the corners to make a square. You can use rope, zip ties, or duct tape to fasten them.
- Cut two more green branches to about 3.5" in length and fasten them to your square making an "X" in the middle. This will provide you with a strong frame for your shower bag.
- Tie a rope to each corner of the frame and have them meet at the top to provide you with a method of hanging the frame.
- Place the now-warm bag on top of the frame and suspend the whole thing from a tree branch so that the frame is just above head-level.
- To allow for privacy, suspend some tarps, blankets, or plastic sheets around your shower area.
- Allow one corner of the filled bag to poke down through the framework—this will be your shower head. Poke a few holes though that part and enjoy your warm shower. Be sure not to poke too many holes or your shower will be over too quickly. If you need to stop the water flow, just fold up the corner and wrap a rubber band around it.

If you are looking for a more permanent solution, then a camp shower is just the trick. Camp showers come in two types—hanging showers and pump showers. Hanging showers work pretty much exactly like the makeshift solution I just described—they will come with a sturdy bag that you fill with water. The water-filled bag then heats up the water by solar power. Hang your bag on a tree branch and shower away. Store-bought camp showers will come with some features that a garbage bag on a frame won't have. The bags are thicker since they are made to be reused. They will typically come with a carrying handle and a method to hang them already attached to the bag. They will come with an attached hose and shower nozzle to make your showering experience a great deal easier than trying to stand under the corner of a bag. Finally, since they are designed to heat the water contained in them, they tend to do that task very well. Many camp showers can heat water to over 100 degrees in just under a couple of hours of direct sunlight. Hanging camp showers are also very reasonably priced and can typically be purchased for $30 or less.

Pump showers work on a similar principle in that they come with a durable bag that you fill with water and the water is heated by solar power. The biggest difference is that pump showers do not need to be suspended from a tree. They come equipped with a foot pump or hand pump which pressurizes the water tank. Now if you've ever used a hand-pumped garden sprayer, you know that you're not going to see a tremendous amount of pressure from this, but it's better than nothing and it can be more convenient than trying to hang a heavy bag from a tree every day. Pump showers can be purchased for around $100.

If price is no object, then there is an additional tier above pump showers—electric pump showers. These are just what they sound like—a pump shower that is powered by some type of battery instead of a hand or foot pump. Higher end models even include the ability to heat the water using LP tanks instead of solar power. You definitely pay for these conveniences as these types of camp showers can cost anywhere from $100 to over $300 although there are arguments that can be made for these. One of the biggest is the simple fact that traditional camp showers heat the water using solar power. If it's cloudy or if the weather is cold already, then you're not going to get much heating happening to your water. The last thing you want when you're already cold is a tepid shower. If you have the budget and you live in an area prone to long interruptions in power or water, then a more high-end electric pump camp shower will definitely provide you with a more pleasurable shower until your regular utilities are restored.

In lieu of a camp shower, there is always the old standby of scented antibacterial wipes. They may not be as effective as a real shower, but they will certainly do in a pinch.

Answering the Call of Nature

We can't really have a discussion about personal hygiene without touching on one very important point—how will you go to the bathroom? The solution to this is remarkably simple, too. Many people are not fully aware of this, but a regular household toilet will still continue to function without power or running water. During a normal flush cycle, the tank of the back of the toilet fills up to a certain level which is defined by a float of some kind. Once the float registers that the water in the tank has reached the appropriate level, the incoming water flow is stopped. This essentially leaves one flush in reserve in the toilet tank even when the water is not running. When you flush the toilet, a flapper in the bottom of the tank opens and the water from the tank flows down into the bowl where gravity pushes the existing water from the bowl down the sewer pipe and out of your house.

All you need to do to have a working toilet is to make sure that there is water in the tank after you flush. This can be water you have collected from a river or stream or collected rainwater if you'd prefer not to have to dip into your supply of drinking water.

This may not be practical for you if your bathroom is damaged or if you don't have extra reserves in your drinking water supply to use to flush your toilet each time. If this is the case, you still have options. A simple toilet can be fashioned using a 5 gallon bucket, garbage bags, and sawdust or kitty litter. Line the bucket with a garbage bag, sprinkle the inside of the bag with sawdust or kitty litter, and conduct your business. Once finished, you just lift the bag out of the bucket, tie the top closed, and dispose of it.

An upgrade to the bucket would be a camp toilet. Camp toilets also come in a range of sizes and features with the more basic models being not much more than an upgraded bucket with a seat. Higher-end camp toilets include features like pressurized water or battery powered flushing systems. Features aside, camp toilets are designed to collect the waste in a tank for later disposal although there are some models that are designed to collect and compost the waste. Expect to pay at least $100 for a camp toilet that is not just an upgraded bucket, with more fully-featured ones being more in the range of $200.

Doing Laundry

With roving bands of the walking dead around, having clean laundry probably isn't going to be the most pressing thing on your mind. Let's face it, with most of the world's population reduced to shambling, rotting corpses things probably aren't going to smell all that great anyway. Of course, the odds are that you are far more likely to be a involved in a natural disaster than the Zombie Apocalypse and, as much as we might not like to admit it, you will still need to go out around other people, get supplies, and probably go to work. So aside from keeping yourself clean, you will also need to keep your clothes clean. So how does that happen with no running water and no power? Obviously your washing machine will be useless in this situation. It is also very likely that you will not have access to a laundromat or dry cleaner. How are you supposed to wash your clothes? The answer to that is by using the methods that your grandmothers or great-grandmothers used and I'll warn you ahead of time—it's slow and labor intensive.

To start off, we need to establish exactly what happens when you wash your clothes now—beyond dumping everything into the washer and pressing a button. Dirty clothes are immersed in water with some type of soap or cleaning agent dissolved in it. The clothes are agitated around in the soapy water. This motion causes the clothes to rub up against each other and other surfaces inside the wash tub. This rubbing action along with the soap and water helps break down stains on the clothes. Once the cleaning cycle is finished, the clothes are then rinsed with clean water to make sure all of the soap is removed. The rinse cycle is followed by the "spin cycle" in which the water is drained from the wash tub and the clothes are spun around at high speed in order to extract most of the water from the clothes by centrifugal force. At this point, the clothes are removed from the washing machine and put into a clothes dryer where they are tumbled around in a large drum while heated air is blown through the drum to fully dry the clothes. Now remove electricity and running water from this equation and you have a slightly different looking process. The basic steps are the same: immerse the clothes in soap and water, agitate them, then dry them.

The work involved is quite different. For the soap and water step, you will need a large tub (although you should preferably have two tubs—one with soapy water and one with clean water to rinse).

Providing the agitation is where the work comes in. Without power, the only way to do this is by hand. The most basic way is by using what is known as a washing dolly or a "dolly stick." A dolly stick is a short wooden pole with a horizontal handle at the top and a surface at the bottom with several wooden prongs attached bearing a passing resemblance to a wooden broom. The dolly stick provides the agitation by plunging it up and down into the wash tub and twisting it around. If that sounds like quite a physical workout, that's because it is. Just think about how long your washing machine runs in a standard wash cycle. Any really stubborn stains require extra measures. This would be where you use a washboard. Typically seen as decoration nowadays, a washboard is a small wooden board with some type of ridged surface (usually zinc or galvanized steel) on one side. Clothes were taken from the soapy water and scrubbed up against the ridges of the washboard to help break up stains.

If you're feeling a little less "DIY" regarding the whole laundry thing, there are several pre-made devices to help with this process. Search for "camp washer" or "hand-powered washer" online or at your local camping supply store. Granted, these devices are designed to be efficient and easy to use, but they still require manual labor. Instead of plunging an agitator, you may be turning a crank, but the energy used to clean your clothes has to come from somewhere!

Now your clothes are clean, but they're still soaking wet. You need to get the excess water out of them to help speed up the drying process. Normally this is the function of the spin cycle on your washer, but if you don't have that luxury then you need to have another method. The most "old school" of methods is to simply wring them out—just twist them and squeeze them until nearly all of the water is out of them. This is very labor intensive and not very efficient since you're relying almost entirely on your hand strength. A good alternative is a hand-cranked clothes wringer. This is essentially two rollers attached to a crank. You turn the crank which turns the rollers. Then you feed your wet clothes through the rollers which squeezes out most of the water. This will leave you with clothes that, while still wet, are no longer soaked and can now be hung to dry.

If you remember your mother or grandmother having a clothesline in their yard, then you are already familiar with this idea because that is exactly where we are going. Your wet clothes are hung up on clotheslines and the sun and wind dry them naturally. Some advantages to this is that it is completely free to use plus your clothes generally end up smelling great. Some disadvantages are the simple fact that it takes time—usually several hours even on the hottest days. Another thing to note is that some items can feel stiff or scratchy after drying them on a clothesline. I have found that bath towels are especially susceptible to this. This happens when certain fabrics dry while being nearly motionless. Drying things in a clothes dryer means they are constantly in motion and tumbling around. Clothes drying on a clothesline are moved around by the motion of the wind, and that's about it.

Clotheslines are obviously only a good choice when it is sunny outside. What about when it's raining or in the winter? In that case, you will need an indoor version of a clothesline—a clothes drying rack (sometimes called a clothes horse). Clothes drying racks are foldable structures that unfold and provide you with places to hang clothes. Other than the fact that they are used inside instead of outside, the principle is exactly the same—hang your clothes on them and wait for them to dry. Without the benefit of the sun and wind, your clothes will take longer to dry inside so plan accordingly.

Getting Around

You're clean. Your clothes are clean. You are presentable enough to be seen in public and your job requires you to come into the office. While getting back to work may not seem like the highest priority for you after a natural disaster, there will come a point when you will need to get back to the normal routine—if for no other reason than you'll probably need to earn some money. Your job could be one of those jobs that other people need done in order for "normal" society to start to function again. Putting the actual reason aside, you are still going to need to be able to get around. Depending on the scale and severity of the disaster, this could be very easy or it could be extremely challenging. If the roads, bridges, and other infrastructure are clean and undamaged, then you will most likely be able to drive. An important point to remember is that if you are in a widespread power outage, gas stations will not be able to pump gas since that requires electricity. Assuming open roads and a full tank of gas, there's not much stopping you from just driving where you need to go.

This can get complicated if the roads are impassible due to heavy snow or flood waters. High winds can blow down large trees across the road which will also make them impossible to traverse in a car. Bridges, overpasses, and other infrastructure items can be damaged or destroyed making your normal route useless. If a route is not drivable by a car, it still could be traversable on a bicycle. Bicycles also have the advantage of not requiring any gasoline to run (since you provide the fuel by expending your energy to pedal). If you bike up to an obstruction in the road, you can also dismount the bike and carry it around (or over) whatever is blocking the road. There will also be times where riding a bike is not feasible. At this point, your only real option is walking. This is also the time to mention that you should be aware of several possible routes to and from your destination since you won't know the conditions of the route until you encounter them. If you need to turn back or circle around an impassible area, knowing the surrounding area could mean the difference between getting where you're going and getting lost.

Keeping Cool

Air conditioning is a marvel of modern life—especially for the places in the country that get very hot. Of course being without power for a prolonged period of time means that you will also be without the benefit of an air conditioner. If a disaster strikes in the middle of summer, you are going to need to find ways to stay cool and remain comfortable.

- Drink plenty of water—Dehydration, heat exhaustion, and heat stroke are just some of the heat-related conditions that can sneak up on you very quickly if you're not properly hydrated. The general rule is that you need about one gallon of water a day, but in hot weather, your body's water needs can double or even triple. Your body cools itself by evaporation—you exert yourself and your body heats up which causes you to sweat and the sweat evaporates off your skin to cool you down. Obviously, the fluid that you sweat out has to come from somewhere. If it is really hot and you're sweating profusely, it is imperative that you drink enough fluids to keep yourself rehydrated. Just like a car engine with a radiator leak—once the cooling fluids run out, it's not long before a serious problem happens. Drinking cold water is not only refreshing when it is really hot, but it also helps cool you down.
- Wear thin, loose-fitting clothing—Since your body cools by evaporation, you will want to dress to allow this to happen. Wearing loose-fitting clothing made of thin, lightweight material will go a long way in helping this process. Loose-fitting clothes allow more of your skin to make contact with the air—which is how sweat evaporates. Clothes made of thin, lightweight material also keep you dryer and cooler for the same reasons. Lightweight fabrics dry very quickly. Natural fabrics such as cotton or linen are very light and breathable and so they are perfect to help keep you cool in the heat. Think about some of the old movies you've seen. When they want to portray people who live in the desert, what are they wearing? Usually long flowing clothes. Contrary to what you might think, wool (specifically merino wool) is another excellent choice. Merino wool has the ability to absorb water and release water vapor very quickly. That means it will behave like many of the "performance" fabrics in that it will absorb sweat, "wick" it away from the surface of your skin to the outside of the fabric, and allow it to evaporate away, keeping you dryer and cooler

in even the hottest of weather. Normally when people think of wool clothes we think of thick wool sweaters in the winter, but athletes have known of the cooling properties of wool for a long time. Before the advent of modern man-made performance fabrics, cycling jerseys used to be made of 100 percent lightweight wool and there are "old school" cyclists still riding today that will swear that a wool cycling jersey will do a better job of keeping you cooler and dryer.

- Light colored clothing—Lighter colored clothing will reflect back most of the light that hits it which, in turn, makes it cooler. Dark clothes absorb the light which causes them to be warmer. It stands to reason that if your clothing is hot, then you are going to be hot. If you're going to spend any time out in the sun, your best practice to stay cool is to wear light colored, loose fitting clothes made of a thin, breathable fabric. Contrary to what you may think, you should keep as much skin covered as possible. Shorts and a tank top may seem like a good idea, but that outfit will leave you with a lot of skin exposed to the heat of the sun. Long sleeves and long pants will do a much better job of keeping the sun off your skin and thus keeping you cooler. Don't just limit yourself to your shirts and pants, though. You will also want to keep the sun off of your head and face. A wide-brimmed hat does a great job of this. Think back to all of the people you have seen wearing wide-brimmed hats. What were they doing? Gardening? Fishing? Probably some type of outdoor activity where they are directly in the sun—and now you know why. Keeping the sun away from your skin will keep you cooler and dryer, but it will also protect you from sunburn. Like so many other things, a sunburn is not an enjoyable experience even when the hungry dead are not roaming the earth, but it can be even more serious without the ready access to medical care we enjoy in "normal" day-to-day life.

While a mild sunburn can be an inconvenience, a more severe sunburn can cause extreme discomfort and blistering of the skin. If a sunburn is severe enough, some people can develop sun poisoning. While sun poisoning is not an official medical term, it is still a real condition. While you're not technically being poisoned by the sun or its UV rays, the combination of the intense pain from the severe sunburn, the shock to your system from the damage done to your skin, and the fact that you are most likely dehydrated as a result leads to some pretty miserable symptoms. Sun poisoning symptoms often mimic those of the flu: headache, fever, nausea, severe chills, and lethargy, but can also include a painful rash, dizziness, confusion, lightheadedness, shortness of breath, and fainting.

- Keep cool with water—There's a reason beaches and pools are so crowded on hot, sunny days—since your body cools itself by the evaporation of moisture from your skin, it just stands to reason that you can help this process along. If you have a pool or have access to a pool, then use it. Aside from feeling refreshed after a dip, the water evaporating away from your skin will help cool you off. If you don't have access to a pool, take a cool bath or shower for the same effect. Just being in the cool water will cool you down although you should fight the temptation to make your bath or shower too cool. The water should be cool, but not cold. If you're in the water and you're shivering, then it's too cold. Shivering is a technique that your body uses to try to warm itself up so that's completely counter to trying to stay cool. If you don't have the luxury of being able to sit around a pool all day, then carry a small spray bottle of water with you and mist yourself occasionally. The mist of water on your skin will evaporate and cool you. Some variations on this would be to leave your hair wet when you come out of the shower. The water evaporating from your hair as it dries will have a similar effect. If this is not practical, then wet a bandana in cool water and wear it on your head or tie it around your neck or wrist. If you find this is not working, then place a cool cloth in your armpit or groin area—those are the hottest areas of the body and so ER doctors will place ice packs there to rapidly cool patients.
- Limit outdoor activity—If you absolutely need to be outside doing something—especially something involving physical activity, then try to schedule your time outside in the cooler parts of the day. Early morning and late in the evening are best. Typically in the summer, the time between 3:00 p.m. and 4:30 p.m. is the hottest part of the day and so you should try to avoid doing any strenuous activities outside during that time.
- Eat early or late—When you eat, your body uses energy to digest the food. Any time that your body does work, it generates heat. When the weather is the hottest, you should try to eat your main meals of the day either very early in the morning or very late at night during the coolest parts of the day. That way the extra energy your body is going to generate by digestion won't heat you up too much.

- Eat cold food—A good hot meal really hits the spot on a cold winter's day but eating hot food when the weather is hot is only going to serve to make you hotter. During warm weather you should eat as much cold food as you can. There is a reason why salads, ice cream, fruit, melons, and the like are popular summer dishes. You should also make an effort to eat smaller portions when it is hot. Since your body generates heat when digesting, smaller, cool meals will go a long way to keep you cool.
- Sleep outside—If you have a secure area to do so, grab your sleeping bag and sleep outdoors on the hottest nights. Even on the hottest days, things cool off rapidly after the sun goes down. If you've never slept outside before, you will probably be surprised at just how cool it can get—which is why I suggested the sleeping bag. If sleeping outside isn't practical for you, try to sleep in an area with plenty of air circulation. Optimally you want to have multiple windows on different walls that you can open so that you can get a cross breeze blowing through. Even a little air blowing can help make the hottest weather more bearable.

As cool as you can keep yourself, it won't do much good if your house is sweltering. Fortunately there are plenty of things you can do to keep a cool house—even in the hottest temperatures.

- Keep the windows covered—Whether you have blinds or shades, keep them closed—especially on the side of the house that faces west. Blocking the sun from getting in will go a long way to keeping the interior of your house cooler. The next step up in protection would be to use heat-blocking curtains. Heat-blocking curtains will block up to 90 percent of the light and so will help insulate against heat. Look for a thermal curtain with at least two layers of triple-woven fabric and blackout technology for maximum effect. Heat blocking curtains are thick so as a side effect they also block out some noise. For a more permanent feature, you could install awnings on your windows. Awnings will provide shade for your windows and reduce the amount of heat coming in. In fact, awnings installed on south facing windows can reduce the amount of solar gain by 65 percent and awnings installed on west facing windows can reduce the amount of solar gain by 77 percent. Solar gain is a measure of the amount of solar radiation that heats an area or simply how much a specific area heats up from the sun. Reducing the overall solar gain in a building means the building will stay cooler. Granted, installing awnings on your windows is something you're going to want to do well in advance of a disaster, but there are other benefits to them as well. Many people prefer the way they look and they do add a certain aesthetic appeal to a house. From a financial standpoint, reducing the solar gain of your house means that your air conditioner will not have to work as hard to cool it down thus saving you money on your cooling bill.

- Close off the warmest rooms—Typically rooms on the west side of your house will be hotter than rooms on the east side for the simple fact that west-facing rooms will get the direct evening sun. If certain rooms of your house are too warm or too difficult to keep cool, just close them off and don't use them. Block off any vents in the rooms, then close the doors. Seal off the doors by stuffing rags under the bottom of the door and sealing off any cracks with tape or plastic sheeting. The idea behind this is to seal as much of the hot air in the room as you can and to keep it from getting into the area that you are trying to keep cool.
- Stay downstairs—Hot air rises so naturally the lower floors of a house are going to be cooler than the upper floors. Seal off the top rooms of your house and move as much of your living space as you can to your first floor or basement.
- Air out your house—Naturally your house will heat up throughout the day. It is sitting in the sun, after all. One trick to help "reset" the temperature in your house is to wait until the coolest part of the day (typically right around dawn), then open all of your doors and windows. If you have fans, use them in the windows as well. The idea is to get as much air flowing as possible to get the hot air out of your house and the cooler night air in. Once your house has cooled down, you can close any blinds and seal off any rooms that were sealed off before. What you are trying to do is to essentially trap the cool outside air in your house. Not only will it feel more comfortable inside, it will also take a little longer to heat back up. Repeat this process every day and you'll be surprised as to what a difference it can make.
- Cool by evaporation—Just like your body cools itself by sweat evaporating off your skin, any wet object will get cooler as water evaporates off it. Your windows are already open so wet a towel or sheet and hang it in front of the window. It will cool the air around it as it dries and the wind blowing past it into your house will cool as well. This is an old trick that dates all the way back

to the ancient Egyptians. Needless to say, they knew how to stay cool in a very hot environment without the benefit of air conditioners!

- Cook outside—If you are without power, you're probably cooking on a camp stove or your grill. If not, you should try to do as much of your cooking as you can outside or at least away from your living area. Before the advent of modern appliances many houses were built with what was known as a "summer kitchen" which was basically a second kitchen either in the basement or in a shed adjacent to the house. Before gas and electric stoves, cooking was done on wood-fired stoves which would naturally generate quite a bit of heat. The summer kitchen was used in hot weather so as to not heat up the house when making meals.
- Battery powered fans—Even on the hottest of days, it feels better to have some air circulating. From a scientific standpoint, the flow of air over your skin helps keep you cooler by allowing more sweat to evaporate. While you can't count on a breeze blowing every day, there are things you can do to help create one. There are battery powered fans in all shapes and sizes. They range from larger fans designed to hang from the ceiling of a tent to smaller fans made to sit on a table. There are even ultra-portable fans designed to be worn on a lanyard around your neck to provide you with a refreshing breeze wherever you go.

Keeping Warm

A prolonged power outage doesn't just mean your air conditioner won't run, nearly all furnaces have some electronic component—even if it is just the mechanism to start it. That means that if your power is out and you plan on sheltering in place in your house, you'll need to find some way to stay warm.

- Dress warm—Naturally, if it is cold in your house, you are going to dress warmly, but be smart about it. Don't just throw on every piece of clothing you have in your closet and hope for the best. The most efficient way to keep yourself warm is to dress in layers. More specifically, you should dress in three layers with each layer having a purpose.
    - ◊ Layer 1—the Base Layer: Your base layer is your first line of defense to help keep sweat away from your skin. The dryer you are—the warmer you are. Also, being damp and cold

opens the door for hypothermia. Your base layer should be a garment that fits close to your skin—snug, but not tight. Having a small layer of air between your skin and your clothing helps act as an insulator and protect you against the cold. Good base layers are T-shirts or a set of thermal underwear. Thermal underwear typically comes in two pieces so you will have a base layer for your legs as well.

- ◊ Layer 2—the Insulating Layer: Your second layer is the layer that will trap in your body's heat and insulate you from the cold. Naturally, the better this layer traps your body's heat, the warmer you will be. Good second layer garments are flannel shirts, wool sweaters, or sweatshirts. For your legs, thick pants, jeans, or even flannel lined pants do an excellent job of keeping you warm.
- ◊ Layer 3—the Protection Layer: This layer acts to protect your other layers from the elements. This is where jackets or coats come in. Jackets, coats, and most other outerwear are designed to (at least partially) block wind, rain, and snow and keep all of your other layers (and you) warm and dry. This layer is obviously where you would put on a jacket, vest, coat, or parka. Snow pants or even a pair of thick sweatpants can act as a final layer for your legs.
- ◊ The Bonus Layer—Staying dry is the key to staying warm. If you need to be out in wet conditions for a prolonged period of time, then a fourth layer of some type of waterproof gear is essential. Dedicated rain jackets and pants are ideal for this since they are water**proof** whereas most other jackets and coats are water **resistant**—meaning that if you are out in the rain or snow long enough, they will get wet. Wet and cold is not just miserable, but it can be dangerous.

- Wear socks and shoes—stepping on a cold surface with bare feet is a surefire way to get cold. Even if your house or apartment has carpet, if the heat is out, it's a good practice to keep your socks and shoes on. If you have wool socks to wear, so much the better. Wool is a fantastic fabric in that it is very absorbent—in fact, it can absorb up to 30 percent of its weight in water. On top of that, wool doesn't get cold and clammy when it gets wet like other fabrics do. Without getting too deep into the science, wool fibers naturally have tiny pockets of air in between them. These pockets give moisture somewhere to go when it is absorbed by the fabric so it doesn't sit right up against your skin. These pockets also allow air to more freely circulate through the fabric which helps any trapped moisture evaporate. Wool, unlike other fabrics, heats up as water evaporates from it. Taking all of this into consideration, it's no wonder that wool has been used for socks and sweaters for years!

- Gloves and hats—Don't be afraid to wear gloves if it is cool enough—even inside your house. Any place that you can avoid losing body heat from skin contact with cold objects is going to be helpful. The same goes for a hat. Manners can take a back seat when you are trying to stay warm so wear your hat inside! There is a common myth that you lose most of your body heat through your head and that is just what that is—a myth. However, your head, like every other part of your body, radiates heat and wearing a hat will help prevent heat loss so it is good practice. Even something as simple as a ball cap will help, although a knit cap or a "watch cap" can be pulled down over your ears, which will definitely make you feel warmer.
- Hand and foot warmers—People have used devices as hand warmers for centuries. Everything from rocks to baked potatoes have been used—anything that can be heated up, store the heat, and release it gradually. Fortunately for us, we now have access to inexpensive chemical hand warmers. These are little packets that contain iron powder, vermiculite (containing water), salt, carbon, and cellulose all of which combine to form a chemical reaction when exposed to air. This chemical reaction produces heat. These chemical hand warmers can produce heat for several hours. They are perfect to tuck inside your gloves or socks and will help keep your hands and feet toasty and warm.
- Bundle up—Any time you are sitting down for an extended period of time, cover up with a blanket. If you have someone with you, then both of you get under the blanket together. Sharing body heat is a great way to stay warm. Don't forget about your pets, either. They're going to be just as chilly as you and would most likely love to share in a warm cuddle session under a blanket.
- Eat and drink regularly—Your body is going to need to spend energy to help keep you warm and that energy has to come from somewhere. Eat and drink on your regular schedule to keep your body supplied with enough energy to do the job. Hot meals are optimal since the warm food will also help warm you up. Room temperature food should be your second choice and cold food should be avoided if at all possible. Eating or drinking anything cold will naturally cool you down—which is not the result you are looking for.

- Exercise—Get up and move around periodically as you start to feel chilly. Moving around will serve to warm you up as your body reacts to the activity you're doing. It doesn't have to be strenuous to be beneficial—do a few pushups, walk around the room, climb the stairs a few times—anything that gets your pulse rate up. Don't do so much that you start to sweat. Sweating is the body's method of cooling down and you're trying to do the opposite. Sweating will also get your clothes wet which is also a bad idea when you are trying to stay warm. Just a few periods of brief physical activity will be good enough to make you warmer.
- Use your car's heater—A quick and easy way to warm up is to spend some time in your car. Start up your car and sit in it for a few minutes with the heater running and you'll be nice and warm in no time. Granted, this solution comes with a few caveats. Naturally you have to have enough gas for your car to be able to start it and keep it running. If you have access to working gas pumps, this is much easier. If you can't fill up due to impassible roads, power outages, or other service interruptions, then you will want to limit your car's use for when it is really needed. Also, your car needs to be outdoors or in a well ventilated area before you do this. Sitting in a running car in a garage with the garage door closed is extremely dangerous. As a car's engine runs, it generates exhaust gases. One of these gases is carbon monoxide which can be fatal in a relatively short time. On a similar note, even if your car is not in a garage you should always make sure your tailpipe is clear if you plan on sitting inside and running it. Heavy snow can accumulate to the point that it blocks the car's tailpipe. Running a car with a blocked tailpipe will have the same effect as running a car in a closed garage—the carbon monoxide generated in the exhaust will have no place to go to dissipate and will slowly fill the car's interior.

Just like there are several things to do to keep your house cool in the hot weather, there are also many things you can do to keep your house warm in the cold weather.

- Generator—It goes without saying that a generator would be very helpful if you have access to one. While a whole house generator will allow you to continue to live pretty much normally without power, whole house generators are expensive and require professional installation—not something you are going to have done in response to a natural disaster. A smaller portable generator can still be very helpful despite not providing enough power to run your entire house. While electric heat is outside of the range of the power that a portable generator can provide, most gas furnaces can be powered by a portable generator. If you are not experienced with electrical wiring, it would be best to have a professional assist you with the nuts-and-bolts of the details, but you essentially want to have a transfer switch installed. A transfer switch is basically a mini–circuit breaker and is typically installed next to your main circuit breaker panel. The transfer switch will connect your main circuit breaker to an outside outlet that you plug your portable generator into. When you lose power, you power up your generator and plug it into the exterior outlet. Inside your house, you flip the transfer switch so that your main circuit breaker is removed from providing power and your generator provides the power. An electrician will assist you so that not only your furnace, but some other outlets in your house will be powered by your generator. This will allow you to run a few devices like lamps, televisions, adapters to charge your phones, or even your wireless router.

- Seal off doors and windows—If you don't have the benefit of a generator, then your first step should be to do what you can to seal the cold air outside. Use plastic sheeting and duct tape to seal off doors and windows. Make the seals as airtight as you can and pay special attention to any large gaps. Large cracks or gaps in outer windows and doors are a nuisance throughout the year since they cause you to have to pay more to heat or cool your house. When you are attempting to regulate the temperature in your house, any place where the cold air can come in is just going to make your task that much harder. Stuff rags into the larger gaps before you cover them with plastic sheets or tape. Add a second layer of protection to this by closing any blinds, shades, or curtains on the doors. In especially cold areas (like the windward side of the house), supplement this by hanging thick blankets over the windows. Blankets also provide excellent coverage for large areas like patio doors.
- Let in as much sunlight as you can—Keeping the curtains closed or covering your windows with blankets will keep the cold air at bay, but natural sunlight can provide significant warming for a house—even on the coldest winter day. If it is at all feasible, try to keep any windows on the south or west sides of your house uncovered. You should still seal them off so the cold air doesn't

creep in, but keep the curtains or blinds open during the day then close them at night or when the sun is no longer shining in. This will maximize the amount of solar gain in those rooms.

- Stay small—It is much easier to heat one small area (such as one or two rooms) instead of a large area (like your entire house). Seal off the coldest rooms in your house and concentrate your living and activities to one or two rooms. These rooms should either be interior rooms or rooms on the southern side of your house. A smaller area will get warm quicker and will be easier to keep warm.
- Stay upstairs—Hot air rises so naturally the top floors of your house will always be warmer than the lower floors. If you're going to hunker down in a room, it should be an upstairs room. Definitely avoid your basement—especially if your basement is partially or fully underground. Soil provides excellent insulation so the cold ground outside pressing up against the concrete walls and floor of your basement will keep them chilly. Couple that with the fact that hot air naturally rises and you get a room that gets cool and stays cool—not where you want to be when you're trying to stay warm!
- Cover bare floors—Tile or hardwood floors are great to look at, but stepping on them with bare feet on a cool morning is a quick reminder of how quickly body heat can be lost to cool surfaces. Throw rugs, area rugs, or even blankets or towels can be placed down to avoid stepping on bare floors.
- Fireplace—Does your house have a fireplace? If so, you will definitely want to put it to use to keep warm. Wood burning fireplaces are the easiest to bring into service for this purpose, but gas fireplaces can work just as well. As long as your gas powered fireplace doesn't have an electric starter, then you can fire it up and keep warm. Even if your gas fireplace has an electric starter, some models have a manual override or a way to start it without using the electric starter. You should consult your fireplace's manual or speak to a professional about that option. Along those lines, it is important to remember that fireplaces (both wood burning and gas powered) require regular maintenance to make sure that they are in good working order and can be operated safely. A fireplace professional will make sure that gas fireplaces are vented properly to ensure there is no buildup of carbon monoxide.

  For a wood burning fireplace, a professional will check your chimney to make sure it is free of obstructions and that there is no buildup of creosote. When you burn wood in a fireplace, the smoke contains small particles of unburnt wood. As the smoke rises through your chimney it cools down, which causes the unburnt wood particles to condense out of the smoke onto the inside of the chimney (also known as the *flue*). This condensation hardens into a substance known as creosote. Creosote is a tar-like substance that can dry into a hard residue. More importantly, creosote is extremely flammable at relatively low temperatures. Creosote can ignite at temperatures as low as 451°F (233°C)—which may seem quite high, but 451°F is the point at which paper burns and a fireplace can certainly exceed that temperature. A buildup of as little as ⅛" (3.2 mm) of creosote in a chimney can ignite and cause a chimney fire. Chimney fires are extremely dangerous as they can very quickly spread to your attic or roof and lead to a full-blown house fire in very short order.

- Space heaters—There are a wide variety of space heaters that can be used to help warm up an area. They come in all shapes and sizes and will typically burn some type of fuel to generate heat with kerosene and liquid propane (LP) being the most popular. Space heaters are very useful in this type of situation since they are portable and can be moved from room to room. They can also be stored away when they are not in use. The fuel for them is inexpensive and readily available—kerosene can be purchased at many gas stations and LP tanks can be purchased at hardware stores and camping supply stores. Space heaters should only be used in well ventilated areas since they produce carbon monoxide as they burn the fuel. Also, since space heaters have an open flame, they should never be left unattended or left to burn overnight while you're sleeping. Caution should be used when positioning them so that they are not placed in an area where they could be bumped into or knocked over.
- Makeshift heaters—There are many normal items that can be used to create improvised heat sources in a pinch.
    - ◊ Take a regular terra-cotta flower pot and turn it over. Place it upside down with the lip of the pot sitting on two bricks. Place a tea light or small candle under the inverted pot and light it. The tea light will warm up the trapped air under the inverted pot and the terra cotta will trap the heat and slowly disperse it into the outside air. This simple heater will provide a surprising amount of warmth in an area for several

hours. If you have a larger pot, then use two or three tea light candles.

- ◊ If you have a working fireplace, gather some bricks or larger stones and place them in the fireplace while a fire is going. Once the fire starts to die down, carefully take the stones out of the fireplace and wrap them in a heavy blanket. Like the terra-cotta pot, the rocks will absorb the heat from the fire and slowly release it. Obviously you want the rocks to be cool enough to be able to safely manipulate them. Pulling a red hot stone from a fireplace and wrapping it in a blanket is a recipe for a fire. Also, use bricks or very dense stones like granite, marble or slate. Lighter more porous rocks like sandstone, limestone, and shale can sometimes have water trapped deep in the structure of the rock. The water will heat up and expand quicker than the material of the rock and can cause the rock to explode with some force.
- ◊ Just like your gas fireplace may still start without power, your gas stove may still ignite without power. If so, then the simple act of cooking or baking something will generate heat and warm up the surrounding area. Boil water on your gas stove, camp stove, or grill and fill up a hot water bottle. Water is an excellent insulator, meaning it traps heat quickly and releases it slowly. Keeping a hot water bottle on you is an excellent way to keep warm. Boil more water and refill when it starts to lose its heat.

- Have an indoor campout—Having already established that it is much easier to heat up a smaller area, why heat an entire room to a comfortable temperature if you don't have to? Take the largest room that you are staying in and move the furniture out of the way (exercise helps keep you warm, remember?). Set up your tent in the center of the room and, just like camping, spend most of your time in the tent. The smaller area inside the tent will be easier to get warm and keep warm. If you have kids, the idea of an indoor campout could add a little fun to a stressful situation, too.

Summary: How Likely Is This to Happen?

Large-scale disasters such as hurricanes, wildfires, and severe tornado outbreaks can affect a large geographic area. An entire city or metropolitan area could be affected by a disaster of this magnitude. While there will very likely be substantial damage to buildings, houses, and other structures that you need to be concerned about, a disaster of this magnitude will also cause severe damage to an area's infrastructure. Roads and bridges will be damaged. Utility poles carrying power, telephone, cable, and other utilities will be damaged or destroyed over a wide area. Municipal water supplies could be disrupted or contaminated rendering them useless. These infrastructure items, when damaged, will take some time to be repaired. It would not be unheard of for these repairs to take several weeks. Even barring natural disasters, other events could require you to be self-sufficient for weeks at a time. During the height of the Covid-19 pandemic, many people were suggested or required to stay isolated in their houses. While services were not disrupted per se, having the ability to remain completely self-sufficient for several weeks was very beneficial during that time.

Rick Grimes and all of the other survivors who lived through the months (and even years) after the outbreak of the Zombie Plague all learned the same lesson you are preparing for in this chapter. Regardless of the size, scale, or duration of the disaster—it will pass. A wildfire may rage through an area, a hurricane could devastate a community, waves of ravenous dead could shamble through—but eventually the crisis will be over and life as you know it will begin to return to normal. Emergency personnel and repair crews will all be working as quickly as possible to get day-to-day life (or even society as a whole) back to the way things were before the disaster struck, but this will take time. In the interim, your life will still continue—meaning you will still need to go to work, your kids will need to go to school, you will still need to procure and prepare food. Things like laundry, personal hygiene, and basic household maintenance will need to continue unabated. While this may seem insurmountable without the advantages of modern conveniences like electricity and running water, the information in this chapter demonstrates that it is not an impossible task with a little preparation.

There are still people alive in America today who grew up in a time before houses had electricity or indoor plumbing. Central heat and air conditioning in houses is also a relatively recent amenity. Many of the conveniences that we take for granted were not always available to people who lived before us and they survived just fine. This is not to say that we should eschew all modern conveniences and go live in a secluded cabin in the woods. I am perhaps the world's biggest fan of our modern lifestyle. However, in order to maintain a mindset of preparedness, we all need to recognize the fact that there could be circumstances in which we would have to live without some of these conveniences for an extended period. Your preparedness for this will make all the difference in how easy that is for you and your family.

CHAPTER 5

To Stay Home or Evacuate

Most of this book up to this point has been centered around the idea of building a stockpile of supplies in your house and hunkering down to ride out a natural disaster or Zombie Apocalypse there. What happens if things don't go that smoothly?

Once a disaster happens and you have established the safety of yourself and your loved ones, then decisions need to be made as to how (and where) the next several hours, days, or weeks are going to be spent. Essentially, will you be staying at home or traveling from where you currently are to your house or leaving your house for another location.

Staying Home

Staying home is the safest and most logical plan of action. First and foremost, all of your supplies that you have worked so hard to build up are already there. You don't need to worry about gathering up food or water nor do you have to worry about transporting your supplies to a new location. Your house is the ultimate in familiar locations so you know how to maintain it and to secure it. If you share a house with small children or elderly family members, then the familiarity of staying in a known location goes a long way to help reduce the stress. Familiar settings are also very helpful for your pets as new locations and situations can be confusing and stressful for them.

Aside from your house, your neighborhood is a familiar place as well. Staying home means you can check on your neighbors to make sure they are safe. If roads are impassible, you might be the only contact some elderly neighbors have with other people. While checking on the well-being of your neighbors is important, you can also pool together resources and skills to help each other through the disaster. Elderly or disabled neighbors may need help repairing broken windows or damage to their house. If someone in your neighborhood is a doctor, nurse, or EMT, they could provide valuable skills in case anyone has medical needs. Surplus food and water can be shared among neighbors. There have been several instances of entire neighborhoods having "block party" style cookouts when there were widespread power outages. Everyone realized that the food in their refrigerators was about to reach an unsafe temperature so people fired up the grills and cooked everything they could. This type of neighborly camaraderie will certainly make a natural disaster less stressful.

Your safest course of action is most likely going to be staying home—more importantly, staying off the roads. Depending on the scope of the disaster, the roads outside your immediate location could be damaged or impassible. Even if the roads are traversable, emergency personnel should have priority. Police, fire, and EMT units will be more mobile after a disaster so keeping the roads clear for them could mean the difference between someone receiving aid in a timely fashion or not.

All that being said, there could be times where it is just not practical for you to remain where you are. If you are in a home with small children or someone who has a serious medical condition and your house is without essentials like heat or water, then you will need to leave. The area that you are in could be under a mandatory evacuation order due to a gas leak or chemical spill. In this case you will be required to leave. A disaster could leave your house damaged to the point that it is not safely inhabitable and so you will definitely want to leave.

Getting Home

A fire, flood, storm, tornado, or Zombie Apocalypse is not likely to occur at a convenient time. Considering how much time the average person spends away from their home (at work, school, running errands, etc.), you need to plan for the eventuality that something will happen when you are not home.

When this happens, like always, your personal safety is your first priority. Once you are safe, make contact with everyone on your emergency contact list. Determine everyone's location and their safety. Use your judgment for each of them as you normally would to determine if they are safe where they are or if they should leave the area and head for a safer location like your house.

At this point, the assumption is that you will be wanting to leave where you are and make your way to the safety and security of your house. For the purpose of planning for this, you should assume that the disaster has caused widespread power outages, water service interruptions, and left some or all of the roads on your route impassible. It is recommended that you pack what is known as a **Get Home Bag** to prepare. A Get Home Bag should contain everything you need to provide you with protection for 24 hours—which should be time enough to get back home. You should keep your packed Get Home Bag in your car or in your desk at work—anywhere that it would be likely that you could be stranded. Why should you pack for 24 hours? If worst comes to worst and you find yourself needing to walk home, that can be quite an undertaking. The average American commutes 16 miles each way to and from work. Your commute may be longer or shorter, but a 16 mile walk is nothing to take lightly. At an average walking speed, a 16 mile walk would take a little over 5 hours—and that is assuming perfect conditions. You might have to find your way home through snow, detouring around damaged bridges, crossing debris-covered roads—and that's not even taking the zombies into consideration!

Get Home Bag Contents

- Backpack—For most of the other situations you find yourself preparing for, you can generally pack your stuff in an old bag. A spare gym bag, a duffel bag, or even a canvas grocery bag will suffice. However, your Get Home Bag should really be a backpack. This will allow you to have all of your supplies with you and have both hands free. Think about having to walk home from work. If it's more than just a few blocks, you're not going to want to be carrying anything.
- Water bottle—You're going to be making your way home on foot, so you're going to want to have water. The most logical way to accomplish this is to have a water bottle in your Get Home Bag with the idea that you will either have access to drinkable water or you will have the ability to purify water to drink. There are a few schools of thoughts on this. One idea is to have a single-walled stainless steel water bottle. This allows you to fill the bottle and then boil the water in the bottle to purify it. While that is an option, another idea would be to either have a water filter or water purification tablets in your Get Home Bag. Water purification tablets are the option that takes up the least amount of room and adds the least amount of weight. Water purification tablets do take some time to work, though. The middle ground here is a water bottle with a built-in filter. These

are available at most places that sell camping supplies. While they are more expensive than a run-of-the-mill water bottle and they come with the added expense of a filter that will need to be periodically replaced, they do offer you a way to get drinkable water with only one item.

- Sillcock key—Also known as a plumber key, a hose bib key, or a spigot key, a sillcock key is a vital item to have if your route home takes you through urban areas. The next time you are at a public building, notice the exterior water spigot. You will see that, unlike the exterior spigot on your house, the one on the building seems to be lacking the handle to turn it on. This is for obvious reasons. In order to turn on the water on a spigot like this, you will need to use a sillcock key. It is an "X" shaped tool that has four different sizes of connectors on each end. One of these will open pretty much any commercial spigot. If your route home has you seeing more offices and businesses instead of trees and streams, then having the ability to draw water from one of those places is a great way to ensure you have access to a supply of clean, drinkable water. Now it is worth noting that you should only do this in the most dire of emergencies. By the strict letter of the law, accessing someone else's water (even for survival purposes) is theft. If you happen to go onto the property of an office complex or business that is closed, then you could also be trespassing as well as utility tampering. Naturally, in the middle of the Zombie Apocalypse or a widespread natural disaster, a single person filling up a single water bottle isn't going to cause much of a stir. Again, the key here is to use this in a real emergency.
- Food—You will want to have one day's worth of food in your Get Home Bag and that food should be calorie dense with a long shelf life. It would also be preferable if your food is light and doesn't take up much room. Given that you are looking at 24 hours, you don't have to be too extravagant. The MREs are certainly an option, but they can be large and bulky. Energy bars, protein bars, or meal replacement bars are a perfect thing to pack. They are small, lightweight, and don't take up a lot of room in your bag. They are also high in calories since they are designed to be eaten in place of a meal. One or two of these should be more than enough.
- Headlamp—At some point during your walk, it will be dark—either you will walk long enough that it will get dark, or it may even be dark when you start. Either way, you are going to want

something to help light your way—if for no other reason than so you can see where you're going. While a normal flashlight would suffice for this, I recommend a headlamp instead. First and foremost, a headlamp will keep your hands free. That may seem trivial, but not having to carry something around in your hands is convenient to begin with and extremely useful as your walk stretches on. Another obvious point is that a headlamp is going to shine its light exactly where you are looking. Your walk home may be over treacherous ground due to fallen branches or other debris. The ability to clearly see exactly where you are putting your feet could mean the difference between making it home safely or falling and injuring yourself along the way.

- Rain poncho—Being wet is bad enough, but being wet and cold can be dangerous. Pack a rain poncho to keep you dry as you make your way home. It's up to you whether you want your poncho to be a neutral color or a high-visibility color—although if your route home takes you down any reasonably busy roads, then a high-visibility poncho is a good idea for safety's sake. You should also make sure your rain poncho is large enough to cover you while wearing your Get Home Bag to help ensure that all of your gear stays dry, too.
- Tarp—A small tarp (4' × 8') won't take up much room in your bag or add very much weight. It can prove its usefulness many times over. A tarp can be used to make an improvised shelter. It can be spread out to provide a dry ground cover. It can be wrapped around your backpack to protect the contents against water damage should you find yourself walking through heavy rain.
- First aid kit—A good first aid kit is a staple in any preparation kit. This doesn't have to be a full-blown trauma kit since you're only looking at roughly 24 hours of self-sufficiency. A small kit with some bandages of various sizes, gauze pads, medical tape, a basic splint, a pair of tweezers, moleskin, lip balm, insect repellant, sunscreen and a small supply of over-the-counter medication (aspirin, acetaminophen, allergy medication, antacids, etc.) will do nicely. A small kit like this won't take up much room nor will it add very much weight to your pack.
- Multitool—Another staple to any pack, a good multitool will provide you with the basic tools you need to do minor repairs. A multitool will also have a knife—which is an invaluable survival tool.

- Paracord and duct tape—Two more items that are at home in any preparation kit, you can never go wrong with having a length of paracord (it's flexible like a bungee cord) and some duct tape. The uses for these items are nearly endless.
- Paper map and compass—You probably know the route to work and home like the back of your hand because you have driven it time and time again. A route looks and feels much different on foot versus driving, though. Add to that the fact that you might have to take detours off your normal route. Roads could be closed due to fallen trees. Bridges could be covered by flood waters. If your route includes any freeways or highways, then you will have to find an alternate way around them since it is against the law to walk on freeways. Power outages will mean streetlights and other lighting sources won't be working and even the most familiar neighborhood will look very different in the dark. Having access to a paper map and compass will allow you to be able to navigate your way safely.
- Pen and paper—A pen and paper is another one of those basic staples for any preparedness kit. The simple ability to write down something or leave a note for someone can prove to be extremely important.
- Signal mirror or whistle—There may come a time when you need to get someone's attention and using something as simple as a signal mirror or whistle can be much more effective than shouting or waving. The light from a signal mirror can be seen over a mile away. Likewise the sound from a signal whistle can be heard about a mile away. Naturally there are situations where one will work better than another. A signal mirror will not be very effective at night, for example. Likewise, a signal whistle only works if other people can hear it. A loud environment will lessen the effect of a signal whistle. Fortunately, you can pack both a whistle and a mirror without sacrificing much room in your bag.
- Personal protective equipment (PPE)—Depending on the nature of the disaster, your walk home could be through smoke, dust, fumes, or other things that can make it difficult (or even hazardous) to see and breathe. Your bag should contain some type of protection for your face, eyes, head, and hands. Your face covering should be something that can cover your mouth and nose. This can be an N95 face mask or something just as simple as a bandana. While a respirator could be beneficial, the added weight and space taken up in your bag isn't worth it. A pair of

lightweight safety goggles will provide you with excellent eye protection. A hat seems like a simple addition, but a hat will help keep your head dry in the rain as well as keeping the sun off your head in the heat. Finally, some kind of gloves are needed to keep your hands safe. If you find you can spare the room (and weight), then a good pair of leather work gloves would be optimal. Otherwise a few pairs of latex gloves will still provide you with protection when you have to put your hands into something that you'd rather not touch.

- Heat source—If you live in an area that sees cold weather, then your Get Home Bag should have some items to ensure you stay warm. The simplest method for this is to pack some chemical hand warmers. Chemical hand warmers are lightweight and don't take up much room in your bag. Slip one into each glove and one into the toe of each shoe and your hands and feet will stay nice and warm for several hours.
- Complete change of clothes—Chances are the clothes you typically wear to work would not be very comfortable or protective if you had to wear them on a long walk. Your Get Home Bag should have a complete change of clothing and the clothing should be appropriate for the weather conditions—which means you're going to have to revisit this as the seasons change so you're not caught with shorts and a T-shirt in the dead of winter or long pants and a sweatshirt in the heat of summer.
- Durable walking shoes—Just like your work clothing is likely not to be helpful on a long walk, the shoes you wear to work are probably not suited for walking any great distance. Pack a pair of hiking boots or comfortable walking shoes. Even if a pair of shoes won't fit into your Get Home Bag, they should be with your bag—either in your vehicle or a desk drawer at work. If your feet are going to be your primary source of transportation to get you home, then you want to make sure that they are taken care of.
- Emergency radio—A small radio with the NOAA weather band will allow you to get information on what is going on in the world around you. Preferably the radio should have multiple power sources such as batteries, solar power, and a hand crank. Many emergency radios can also be used to charge your cell phone, which is a nice added bonus since that is one less item you will need to pack.
- Personal protection—In a disaster you will be surrounded by people who are experiencing intense amounts of stress. Remember that most people are not going to be as prepared as

you are and so they could be confused and frightened by what is going on around them. These emotions can make seemingly normal people behave in unexpected ways. The bottom line is you need some way to protect yourself in case you get into a bad situation. Depending on your comfort level, any specialized training you might have, and local laws and regulations, your preferred method of self-protection could vary widely. At minimum a small canister of pepper spray is a very useful addition to your Get Home Bag. Pepper spray doesn't require any special training or even a great amount of skill to use—simply point it at the threat and squeeze the trigger. Pepper spray is non-lethal and doesn't cause any permanent damage, but it provides a very effective deterrent to a threat that will buy you enough time to extricate yourself from the situation. It is also important to note that pepper spray works to repel both people and animals, making it useful if your route home goes through either a more urban or more rural area.

- Cash—Your Get Home Bag should have some cash in small bills. In a widespread power outage, businesses may still be open, but they will not be able to process credit card transactions and ATMs will not function without power. Having some cash on hand will still give you the ability to make purchases as needed.

While this may seem like a daunting list, everything can still be packed into a regular sized backpack. This makes your Get Home Bag not only easy to carry, but easy to store.

Leaving Home

All of the preparation you have made up to this point was centered around stockpiling supplies in your house and hunkering down there—whether you started the situation there or found your way back there. Unfortunately, there is a chance that the safety and security of your home will be compromised and you will have to leave. The zombie horde could overrun your defenses and break into your home. A hurricane could tear the roof from your house. A tornado or a strong storm could cause significant damage. Natural disasters aside, this could be caused by something like an accident. It is not uncommon for construction crews to inadvertently hit a natural gas line while they are working. Any of these situations would cause you to have to leave the safety and security of your house—sometimes with very little notice. A perfect example of this is the opening scene in the 2004 remake of *Dawn of the Dead*. In the film, Ana and Luis are asleep in bed in their house in the suburbs. Luis is awakened by someone standing at the door of their bedroom. He is surprised to find one of the neighborhood girls there and he is even more surprised when the zombified kid attacks him. Luis is killed by the zombie girl and immediately reanimates and attacks Ana. Ana is left with no choice but to immediately flee. This serves to reinforce the point that regardless of how prepared you are, there could come a time when you will need to leave your house and quite possibly leave with short notice.

When this happens, you will need two very important things. First off, you will need a destination. Leaving your house logically means you are headed somewhere. In *Dawn of the Dead*, Ana did not have a clear destination in mind. Granted, she did just witness some pretty traumatizing things and she continued to watch the Zombie Apocalypse unfold around her as she drove. Ana ended up getting into an accident and fortunately was rescued by some other survivors.

Secondly, you will need some way to replicate some of the supplies and preparedness you have in your house. This is where a well-stocked Go Bag comes into play. Both of these concepts will be expounded on in this section.

Where to Go

The inevitable has happened. Your night is interrupted by a frantic knocking on your door. The authorities are there and they're telling you that you need to evacuate immediately. Let's face it, that is a much more palatable scenario than watching your spouse being killed and reanimating as a zombie intent on killing you. The end result is the same, though, you are leaving your house and you are leaving NOW. So, where do you go? Like so many other situations, there is not one answer that will always be correct. You will need to plan for several eventualities. The most important thing to consider is to know your destination **before** you leave your house. By the time you are loaded into your car and turn the ignition key, you should already know where you are going.

The worst thing you can do is to get in your vehicle and just start driving aimlessly around. At best, your random driving is going to contribute to traffic and potentially congest the roads in a time where police, fire, and other emergency vehicles need to be able to travel. At worst, you could get lost or turned around and become stranded or involved in an accident thus adding to the problem and compounding the danger for you. Remember everything you have learned up to this point. Your personal safety is your first and foremost goal. If you get into an accident and injure yourself, you have just become part of the problem instead of contributing to the solution.

If the disaster is limited to your house or a few houses in your neighborhood, then your evacuation plan could be as simple as driving to a hotel in your town and staying there a few days. If the scope of the disaster is larger, then you might need to go farther away to reach a safe spot. At this point, you should consider a hotel in another city or possibly traveling to some out-of-town friends or relatives in a different city (or possibly a different state). Get to a point where you are safe and begin calling the people in your Family Emergency Plan. First, you want to establish their safety and reassure them of yours. Secondly, they might be able to help you. If the disaster is limited to your house or your neighborhood, someone in your Family Emergency Plan might be able to offer you a place to stay—even if it is only for a night.

While it is important to have several possible evacuation sites planned out, it is also important to know several alternate routes to them. When you set out, you won't know the condition of the roads on your route. A severe enough disaster could damage bridges and overpasses. Roads could be rendered impassible by fallen trees or other storm debris or covered by flood waters. Your alternate routes should be planned to avoid as many freeways, bridges, overpasses, tunnels, and other major pieces of infrastructure as possible. Depending on the scope of the disaster, bridges, overpasses, and tunnels could be damaged or not usable whereas freeways could be crowded with other people fleeing the area. If you're trying to quickly evacuate an area, the last thing you want is to be stuck in a traffic jam on the freeway.

If the disaster is of a large enough scale, then federal and other disaster relief organizations will have emergency shelters set up as an option as a safe and secure place to go.

Generally FEMA (the Federal Emergency Management Agency) will be among the first on the scene of a large natural disaster setting up shelters and providing relief and recovery operations. When FEMA sets up operations in an area after a natural disaster, they begin by setting up what is known as a Disaster Recovery Center (DRC). The DRC is essentially a portable headquarters for FEMA in the area. The DRC will have information on the location of FEMA shelters, how to get there, and what help can be provided when you arrive. To locate the closest FEMA DRC, text **DRC** and your ZIP code to 43362 (for example, **DRC 44087** will return the location of the DRC closest to the 44087 ZIP code). You can also text the word **SHELTER** and your ZIP code to 43362 to find the location of the closest FEMA emergency shelter. FEMA will not be the only agency onsite in a widespread disaster. The American Red Cross also provides similar support. The Red Cross website and the Red Cross mobile app will show you the location of the closest Red Cross shelter.

If the time comes that you need to go to an emergency shelter, there are a few points to keep in mind. First off, alcohol, firearms, and smoking are not permitted in shelters. Pets are not allowed in shelters, either (although by law service animals are permitted). Even though pets are not permitted in shelters, bring your pets with you when you evacuate. Most relief organizations will have arrangements made with local veterinarians and animal shelters to provide a safe place for evacuated pets. If you want to be sure what to do with your pet in the case of a mandatory evacuation, talk about it with your veterinarian on your next visit. They can provide you with information on local emergency shelters or other options for your furry loved ones.

It is also worth remembering that emergency shelters will likely be crowded and the people there will have just gone through the same devastation you have. They will not likely be as prepared for this eventuality as you have been and so will be experiencing the worst day of their lives. Needless to say that the other people in the shelter will be under an extreme amount of stress and stress can affect people differently. There's not much you can do to prepare yourself for the reactions and behavior of other people other than to mentally prepare yourself for the situation you will be in.

Packing a Go Bag

A Go Bag or Bug Out Bag is a vital thing to have when you are looking at the possibility of having to leave the safety and security of your house. A Go Bag is, in essence, a bag containing everything you need to be able to comfortably survive away from your house for anywhere from 24 to 72 hours. The idea is to keep your Go Bag fully packed and ready to grab and go so you don't have to spend time gathering supplies from your house when you should be evacuating. Once stocked, your Go Bag should be kept somewhere handy like by your bed, in a hall closet, or even right by the front door—that way when the situation comes where you need it, you can grab your Go Bag as you're headed out the door and be out of the house in minutes while still having all of the supplies you need to spend two or three days away if necessary.

So how do you assemble a Go Bag and ensure you have everything you need? It may seem like a daunting task, but (like many other of the preparations in this book) it is fairly simple and logical. Think of it as a portable, three-day version of all of the preparation you have done to this point.

Packing Your Go Bag

- A bag—Obviously the first place to start is a bag to put everything in. Some people prefer a large duffel bag since it gives them more room. I personally prefer a backpack primarily because it is much easier to wear a backpack for hours at a time than to keep up with a large duffel bag. Using a backpack also forces you to travel as light as possible. This has the benefit of requiring you to consider the value of every item you put into the bag and will keep you from overpacking or packing gear that you really don't need. You want the bag to be made of a thick, durable fabric and some type of water resistance is beneficial. Backpacks by default fit into that category. Each person in your household should have their own Go Bag. This allows each person to tailor the contents of the bag to their individual needs. It also prevents any one bag from becoming too heavy. Small children should also have their own bag for the same reason, but a parent will most likely be keeping up with it for them.
- Emergency contact list—You should have a printed copy of your emergency contact list with cell phone, landline, and alternate contact information for all of the important people in your life. Having an electronic copy of this information is great, but there are many things that can prevent you from being able to access an electronic copy whereas a piece of paper doesn't take up much room in a bag, nor does it add any weight.
- Important documents—In an earlier chapter, we discussed the benefit of an electronic copy of all of the important documents in your life. Definitely keep a copy in your Go Bag. The USB flash drives are inexpensive and some manufacturers even make them that are waterproof for extra safety. If you are not at home and have no access to your house, then you will need some way to get to the information in these documents.
- Water bottle—Water is vitally important to survival. You are not going to have enough room to carry enough water to sustain you for three days, so an empty water bottle is the next best thing.

Somewhere in your travels you will find water that is either safe to drink or can be made safe to drink.

- Water purification—Considering the source, the water that you find may or may not be safe to drink. Ground water (streams, lakes, etc.) should always be purified before drinking—no matter how clean it may look. Given that you are concentrating on packing to travel light, the two best options for this are to either pack some water purification tablets or to have a water bottle with a water filtration device built in. If you live in a more urban area, then you might not have access to many rivers or streams for water. In this case, you should have a sillcock key in your Go Bag. Nearly all public buildings have an exterior water spigot, but instead of a normal handle to turn them on and off, a sillcock key is required to open them. If you see more buildings than trees in your area, then a sillcock key will allow you to access clean, drinkable water from any of those buildings. If you will be more likely to get water from a natural source like a creek or river, then water purification tablets or a water bottle with a filtration device built in will better suit your needs.
- Food—You will need to have a three days' supply of food. In order to conserve as much weight as possible, the food you pack should be calorie-dense, lightweight, and have a long shelf life. The best product for this would be some type of emergency ration bars. These bars are small and very calorie-dense and they are generally sold in vacuum-packed packaging that provides them with an extremely long shelf life. Three days' worth of emergency ration bars will tuck nicely into a backpack and may only add a pound or so of weight. While more varied in flavor, MREs are larger and heavier. They also do not have as long a shelf life. Freeze dried foods are extremely light and has a shelf life literally measured in decades, but they require water (and preferably boiling water) to reconstitute them to an edible state so they are much less convenient than emergency ration bars for a Go Bag.
- Radio—Communication is key and being able to find out what is going on in the world around you is imperative. Your radio should be small enough to pack without trouble and it should be capable of receiving transmissions on the NOAA Weather band. A radio with multiple power sources is a plus. Several manufacturers currently make small emergency radios that are powered by batteries, but can also be charged by solar power and by a hand crank.

- Cell phone battery pack—For most people, their cell phone is their most direct connection to their loved ones. Even taking the most drastic battery saving precautions, your cell phone will not last three days. A battery pack capable of recharging your cell phone will allow you to have a working phone for the duration of the time you're living out of your Go Bag. Naturally, a cell phone battery pack is going to need to be charged to be of use. If you have an outlet close to where you store your Go Bag, then keep it plugged in there so it is ready to grab when you grab your Go Bag and head out the door. Otherwise, schedule regular times to take the battery pack out of your Go Bag and charge it. I personally have a calendar reminder set to notify me on the first Saturday of each month. When I see the notification, that serves as a reminder to me to remove the cell phone battery pack from my Go Bag and plug it in for a few hours. That way I never have to worry about it not having a sufficient charge when I need it.
- First aid kit—The first aid kit you pack in your Go Bag won't be as complete as the one you have prepared at your house, but you only need to be able to provide basic first aid for a few days or until you can get professional medical help. A smaller kit naturally weighs less and takes up less room in your bag. While you could probably get by with an off-the-shelf prepackaged first aid kit, I have found that spending a little time making a custom kit helps you tailor it to your specific needs and prevents you from carrying around items you will never use. Most first aid kits come with a breathing mask to aid in giving rescue breaths during CPR. Many CPR classes now are taught using a "hands-only" technique and forgoing rescue breaths, thus rendering this piece of equipment irrelevant. Preparing your own first aid kit also gives you firsthand knowledge of everything that is in the kit and where it is. In an emergency, you won't have to waste precious seconds wondering if you have a particular item or rummaging around to find it. My recommendations for a good versatile kit would include:
    - ◊ Adhesive bandages—Your basic adhesive bandages will probably get used more than anything else. Pack a few of each size—small, medium, large, fingertip, and knuckle.
    - ◊ Gloves—Any time you're touching bodily fluids, you should be wearing gloves. Nitrile gloves are perfect for this. I recommend two pairs. That way you have a backup pair if

you cut or puncture a glove or if you need a second pair of hands to assist you.

◊ Gauze pads—2" × 2" and 4" × 4" are the most common sizes. Two of three of each size should suffice.
◊ Butterfly bandages—Also known as "steri-strips," these can be used to help close larger wounds that would normally require stitches. They are packaged similar to normal adhesive bandages, so pack several.
◊ Triangular bandage—A triangular bandage can be used as a large dressing, to secure a large dressing in place, or as a sling. Your kit should include one.
◊ Hemostatic agent—This is just a fancy name for something that helps a bleeding wound clot quicker. There are several of these on the market and they run the gamut of bandages and gauze pads with a clotting agent impregnated in them to a powder that you literally pour into an open wound. One packet of the powder and a few of the gauze pads should be all you need.
◊ Self-adhesive bandages—A self-adhesive bandage (or a cohesive bandage—"coban" for short) is a type of bandage or wrap that sticks to itself (coheres) instead of sticking to other surfaces. Usually sold in rolls, cobans can be used to cover wounds, to help hold a coverage on a wound (a gauze pad, for example), and even to provide support or reduce swelling. Since cobans don't stick to skin or cloth, they are a quick and easy way to dress a wound.
◊ Rolled gauze—Rolled gauze is used to secure a dressing to a wound—especially on extremities or near joints where there is a lot of movement. Pack one small roll.
◊ Israeli bandage—A combination of a wound dressing, a hemostatic agent, and the ability to administer direct pressure with the added benefit of being designed so that an individual can use this on themselves if need be, an Israeli bandage is a must-have in any first aid kit.
◊ Tourniquet—If you have training on the correct use of a tourniquet, then definitely pack one in your first aid kit. If you don't have the training, then get trained and pack one. If you have an injury serious enough to require a tourniquet, then having one versus not having one could mean the difference between life and death.
◊ Chest seal—A quick and easy thing to use to prevent a serious injury. A chest seal is a wound dressing with a strong adhesive on one side. It is designed to create an airtight seal

when it is applied. A deep puncture wound on the upper part of the torso has the potential to puncture a person's lung. A chest seal is designed to be applied right over a wound. The adhesive forms a seal and prevents any air from entering the wound. Application of a chest seal can mean the difference between a collapsed lung and being able to breathe. The prevalent thought is to apply a chest seal to any upper torso wound that you think may have punctured a lung. Since they are as simple as opening the package, removing the backing from the adhesive, and sticking it on, chest seals can be used by anyone—even someone with limited first aid training. You should have at least one chest seal in your kit.

◊ SAM splint—A quick and easy way to make a splint, a SAM splint should also be in every first aid kit. For the sake of portability, many people will take a regular SAM splint, unroll it, and cut it in half. This allows you to reroll one half of the SAM splint into a smaller roll. It is still large enough to be effective as a splint, but it takes up much less room in your first aid kit.

◊ Antibiotic cream—Infections are always a concern, but they are more of a concern when you are on the move away from your house and you might not be able to give any wounds the same amount of care as you normally would. One small tube of antibiotic cream in your first aid kit will allow you to treat most of the injuries you will encounter and not have to worry about an infection setting in.

◊ Burn pads—Burns are painful and can be especially prone to infection. Covering a burn with a burn pad will not only help the burn heal quicker, covering the burned area will keep it clean and greatly reduce the chance of its getting infected. Burn pads can also be used to cover and protect cuts, scrapes, and bites. If you can find burn pads in multiple sizes, then pack two large and two small. If you can only find them in one size, then pack two large pads.

◊ Moleskin pads—If you're surviving out of your Go Bag, then chances are you are walking more than you normally would. That is a recipe for blisters, and blisters (aside from being painful) can cause serious problems. Once a blister bursts, the skin underneath is raw and unprotected (as it is essentially an open wound) and so can very easily get infected. Moleskin pads help prevent you from getting blisters by reducing the friction that causes them. Place moleskin pads anywhere you start to feel repeated friction starting to cause problems. It doesn't have to be just your feet, either. Blisters can occur anywhere that your skin is constantly rubbing up against some other substance—like the shoulder straps of your Go Bag.

◊ Antibacterial wet wipes—If you're living out of your Go Bag, then you might not have the opportunity to take regular showers. Having antibacterial wet wipes in your first aid kit will not just allow you to clean any wound areas you have, but also to keep your face and hands clean.

◊ Eye drops—Depending on the type of disaster, there could be smoke or dust in the air. Even on the most pleasant of summer days, the pollen in the air can cause some people to have dry, scratchy eyes. Pack some type of eye drops in your first aid kit to help alleviate this because you can't be expected to get around if you can't see.

◊ Sunscreen—While it would be nice if natural disasters only happened on bright sunny days, that isn't always the case. Bright sunny days can bring about their own types of problems, though. If you are spending any time in the sun, you should be wearing sunscreen. Sunburns and sun poisoning can be very serious problems that can easily be avoided by regular application of sunscreen. A travel-sized tube of sunscreen will fit perfectly in your first aid kit.

◊ Anesthetic swabs—Manufactured under names like "Sting Kill," these swabs are used to provide relief from bee, wasp, and hornet stings. Spending more time outside means spending more time with things that live outside. Bee stings are never fun and these anesthetic swabs do a great job at relieving the pain and itching from bee stings or any other biting or stinging insect. These are very small and compact so you can easily fit three or four into your first aid kit. It is also worth noting that if you or anyone in your family is allergic to bee stings, then an EpiPen is essential for your first aid kit.

◊ Over-the-counter medication—Your first aid kit should have a few different types of over-the-counter medication. Aspirin, a non-aspirin pain reliever like acetaminophen, ibuprofen for pain and swelling, and some antacid tablets are among the essentials. All of these can be found in single-dose packages or you can just slip a few of each pill into a small zip lock baggie. I would recommend at least one day's dosage of each type of medication.

- ◊ Prescription medication—If you take any prescription medication, then you will need to pack enough to last three days in your first aid kit.
- ◊ Medical shears—In an emergency, you might need to cut through thick clothing or bandages. A pair of medical shears makes quick work of this task.
- ◊ Tweezers—A good pair of tweezers is invaluable should you need to remove a splinter or an insect's stinger.
- ◊ Safety pins—Keep three or four safety pins in your first aid kit. They are another item that can prove very valuable if you need to secure a bandage or fashion a sling.

- Flashlight—Whether you choose to pack a standard flashlight or a headlamp is a personal preference, but you can be certain that you will be navigating at some point in the dark or very low light condition and some type of light is essential.
- Chemlights—As a backup to your flashlight, pack a few chemlights or glow sticks. These are small and lightweight, but can provide hours of bright light. Chemlights can be seen up to a mile away and so provide you with some safety. If you are walking in the dark, activate a couple of chemlights and clip them to the outside of your Go Bag. Not only will they give you some more light to see by, but they will also make you much more visible.
- Emergency blanket—Mylar blankets are cheap and lightweight, and they don't take up a lot of room when they are packed. You should have at least one in your Go Bag.
- Pen and paper—When you are living out of your Go Bag, you could be on the move a lot. The ability to write something down—either as a note for yourself or to leave a note for someone else—cannot be undervalued. A pen and a small pad of paper should always be present in your Go Bag. For the ultimate in functionality, the paper should be waterproof and your pen should either be a waterproof pen or permanent marker (or both).
- Paper map—There are a plethora of reasons why a paper map is important. You might not have the benefit of being able to navigate via your cell phone's GPS. You might not even have the advantage of your car. Streets and neighborhoods look much different on foot than they do from a car window. Add to that the fact that you might end up having to take a detour

(or several detours) forcing you to travel through unfamiliar territory. Having a paper map could be the difference between reaching your destination and getting lost and becoming part of the problem.

- Compass—Having a paper map is only part of the navigation process, but even the best map is no good if you don't know which direction you're going. During the day, you can navigate by the sun (assuming the sun is not obscured by clouds or smoke), but you might want to (or need to) travel after dark. Either way, a good compass is an essential navigational tool.
- Signal whistle/signal mirror—Much more effective at getting attention than yelling and waving your arms, a signaling device can be heard or seen over a mile away. Signal whistles are best in quiet environments and signal mirrors obviously work best during the day. Your Go Bag should have one of each to ensure you have the correct signaling method when you need it.
- Toiletries—A travel toothbrush with some travel-sized toothpaste, deodorant, and shampoo are important to have so that, regardless of everything that is going on, you can still feel clean. Women should also pack any necessary feminine hygiene products.
- Change of clothing—Pack a complete change of clothes and make sure the clothes are weather-appropriate. Naturally this will mean that you will need to change out your extra clothes for summer and winter. To save space, compression "stuff sacks" used for travel make for an excellent way to pack clothing and not take up much room in your Go Bag. Your change of clothes should also include a hat. A lightweight, wide-brimmed hat will protect your head and face from the sun in the summer, while a warm hat like a knit cap will keep your head warm in the winter.
- Face/eye protection—In order to safely reach your destination, you need to be able to see and breathe. The air could be filled with dust, ash, smoke, or other things. Your Go Bag should have a pair of safety goggles to protect your eyes and some type of covering for your mouth and nose. An N95 respirator mask is the best option, but even something as simple as a bandana that you wrap around your mouth and nose will suffice.
- Gloves—You never know what you might have to put your hands on, so pack a pair of gloves. A pair of thick canvas or leather work gloves will protect your hands if you need to move debris. They can also keep your hands warm in the cold weather.

- Cash—As always, you should be prepared for widespread power outages, no functioning ATMs, and what business you find open operating on a "cash only" basis. Between $50 and $100 in small bills should provide you with enough resources to make purchases along the way.
- Multitool—You are not going to have the space, nor will you want to dedicate the weight, to carrying around multiple tools. A good multitool will be small and light and still provide you with some of the most important tools you might need. There are multitools with a wide array of features at a wide range of prices. At minimum you will want a knife blade, small saw, Phillips screwdriver, regular screwdriver, and pliers.
- Paracord—Paracord (like bungee cord) is one of the survival essentials. The ability to tie something down, strap something together, replace a broken strap, replace a broken belt, or even replace a shoestring is incredibly handy. To maximize usefulness while minimizing space, pack about 20' of paracord in your Go Bag.
- Duct tape—Another survival essential, duct tape is nearly limitless in its usefulness. To avoid the space needed by carrying around an entire roll of tape, you can wind several feet of duct tape around a piece of plastic like an expired credit card or the body of a pen. Camping supply stores also sell smaller, more portable rolls of duct tape.
- Trash bags—Trash bags are nearly as useful as duct tape in a survival scenario. While you can always use them for their intended purpose, they can also be used as a makeshift rain poncho, improvised gloves, or personal shelter. They can even be used for something as simple as to provide you a dry place to sit on damp ground. Pack two or three large contractor bags in your Go Bag.
- Tarp—Tarps come in many different sizes, but a smaller one (in the range of 5' by 7') can be folded flat enough to pack easily in a Go Bag. A tarp is perfect for making a shelter if you need to stop for a while. You can fashion a perfectly functional lean-to or small tent with just a tarp and some paracord which eliminates the space and weight taken up by trying to pack a tent.
- Sewing kit—A small, travel-sized sewing kit is just what you need to make on-the-go repairs of rips, torn seams, or lost buttons. Even if you're not skilled, pack a sewing kit. In an emergency, you need your gear to work for you. If you are

walking through woods or downed trees and tear a hole in your jacket, the ability to sew the tear closed to keep the cold and rain off you will be much more important than whether or not your stitches are perfect.

- Hand/foot warmers—These chemical hand and foot warmers do an excellent job. They provide heat for several hours and are small enough to tuck into a glove or the toe of a shoe. If you live where it is cold, you should have 8–10 of these in your Go Bag.
- Firestarter—The necessity of your needing to make a fire is going to depend greatly on where you live. If you live in a more urban area, then the odds of your having to build a fire to keep warm are going to be pretty slim. Chances are you will use your Go Bag to get you from your house to some type of shelter and you won't likely be required to spend the night outside in the elements. If, however, you live in a more rural area, then your odds increase of potentially having to spend one or more nights outside. You can fashion a shelter with a tarp and keep warm with an emergency blanket, but at some point you will need to make a fire. If this sounds like your situation, then you will need to pack some type of firestarter in your Go Bag. Fortunately, you have many choices. A disposable lighter, waterproof matches, or a ferro rod (a rod that makes sparks when stuck with metal like a knife blade) are all valid choices and none of them take up too much room.
- Personal protection—Like it or not, you will need to be mindful of your and your family's safety during your evacuation. You will be around people who are experiencing some of the worst days of their lives and they will be under tremendous stress. In all likelihood, they will not be as prepared for the situation as you are and the stress of the situation may cause them to act in ways that they might normally never act. Personal self-defense takes many forms, but the easiest and most readily available is pepper spray. A container of pepper spray can easily slip inside or clip to the outside of your Go Bag so you have it quickly accessible. If worse comes to worst, a blast of pepper spray will make an assailant reconsider their actions long enough for you to extract yourself from the situation. It is also worth noting that pepper spray is also an effective deterrent for many wild animals so it is a good addition to your Go Bag even if you expect to see more trees than buildings during your evacuation.
- Pet supplies—If you're leaving, then your pets are probably coming with you and they have the same survival needs as you

do. Many pet food manufacturers make freeze-dried pet food. Just like freeze-dried human food, freeze-dried pet food is light, it doesn't take up a lot of space in a Go Bag, and it has a shelf life measured in decades. Reconstitute it with a little water and your pet will be eating just like they were at home. It is also good practice to pack an extra collar and leash in your Go Bag just in case you leave home without yours or it gets damaged. A collapsible water bowl is a handy thing to have as well.

- Entertainment—Pack something to occupy your time. This can be a novel, a book of crossword puzzles, or even a deck of playing cards. While a disaster can be initially chaotic and having to leave your house on little notice can be upsetting to your life, you would be surprised at just how quickly things can settle into a routine. One thing in this routine that many people don't think about is just how much time you're going to spend simply waiting. Emergency shelters and other rescue programs will have lines of people. Once you get settled in the shelter, there will be a lot of time to sit around and wait. Having something familiar to occupy your time will help ease the tedium.

Once your Go Bag is assembled, place it somewhere in your house that is easily accessible. You don't want to constantly be moving it or tripping over it, but you also don't want it buried in the back of your guest room closet when you need to grab it and go. You should also check the contents at least once a year. My recommendation is to completely unpack it and repack it. This helps you refamiliarize with what you have in there and where it is stored. It also allows you to test equipment and replace anything that needs replacing. Batteries in devices should be replaced once a year regardless of what the advertised shelf life is. Foodstuffs have "best by" dates. This also gives you the opportunity to examine the bag itself. Is it damaged? Does it need to be repaired or even replaced? Your life circumstances can change—maybe you adopted a dog since you last looked at your Go Bag contents and need to modify them to include your new addition. Ultimately you want everything in your Go Bag to be ready in case you need to use it.

Summary: How Likely Is This to Happen?

How likely is it that you are going to experience a natural disaster at some point? Statistically, it is very likely. Of course, we've already established that the Zombie Apocalypse is not something that you need to worry about. There are fires, floods, strong storms, tornadoes, hurricanes, blizzards, and that doesn't even include man-made disasters like chemical spills, civil unrest, acts of terrorism, and mass shootings. If something happens when you are at work, you probably will want to go home. If something affects your house, you will definitely want to leave. The idea behind both a Get Home Bag and a Go Bag is that you hope for the best but prepare for the worst. You could very well go through all of the time and effort to make the perfect Go Bag and then never use it—and that's great! Honestly, knowing that you have it will bring you great peace of mind. However, if you ever are unfortunate enough to need it, knowing you have everything in a bag that you can just pick up and leave with will drastically reduce the stress of an unquestionably stressful situation. While it sounds like a prepper's fantasy, even FEMA is now recommending that people put together a Go Bag.

Epilogue

Let's face it, nobody ever wants to be in a natural disaster, but they happen all the time and they can happen anywhere. Big cities, small towns, places on the coast, places way back in the mountains—there's nowhere you can go that you won't be subject to the possibility of some type of disaster. If you add in the possibility of being affected by some type of service interruption (either man-made or weather-related), then it's safe to say that you will experience this. In fact, you've probably experienced one already.

The idea behind preparing yourself, your family, and your house for a natural disaster is generally not on the top of many people's "to-do" list. Taken at face value, it's not very exciting. Who really gets worked up about shopping for dehydrated food and stockpiling water? Probably not many people. People are often hesitant to even think about the idea of something horrible like a tornado tearing through their town or a fire damaging their house. Certainly nobody wants something like that to happen, but things like that do happen every day and you want to make sure you and your family can survive safely. The worst thing you can do in a disaster is to do nothing. Conversely, any kind of plan is better than no plan at all. You can plan for what you think is every possible eventuality, but something will always surprise you. That's no reason to not make a plan. In fact, the better you plan the better able you are to react to those surprises that come up.

That is the primary reason this book is written the way it is. You probably picked it up because you like horror movies or at least zombie movies and you've probably watched more than a few of them and thought "Are those people crazy? I'd never do it that way." Framing the idea of preparing for a disaster around the idea of preparing for the Zombie Apocalypse gives you something more interesting and less threatening to work with. Zombies aren't real, after all. Natural disasters, on the other hand, are all too real. Sometimes taking the actual threat out of the situation makes it easier to deal with the reality of it.

There have been studies published that show that people who enjoy watching horror movies do better in natural disasters. Watching horror movies gives our brains a harmless and non-threatening way to work through stressful situations. You know the zombies or the escaped maniac on the screen aren't real and pose no real threat to your safety.

This can provide your brain with a "test run" of being in danger and gives you the opportunity to formulate a response to the threat. This also allows you to think through potential life-threatening situations without your life actually being in danger. Naturally, this provides a calmer and more detailed thought process. It is similar to why recruits in the armed forces go through Basic Training or why emergency personnel often train in loud and chaotic situations. If you can complete tasks under simulated stress, then you are more apt to be able to complete the tasks in a real emergency. Training and practice is important because you never want your first time doing something to be under stress. As stress levels increase, a person's ability to think calmly and rationally decreases.

Preparing for a natural disaster is a detailed process, but as I have tried to demonstrate in this book, it is not an insurmountable process when broken down into smaller chunks. This lessens the time and expense needed to gather enough supplies. A slow planning process also helps to ensure your plans are complete. Even a small bit of preparation will help. You don't have to accomplish everything in this book at once. Having a plan and preparation in place gives you a great deal of satisfaction, but it also gives you the peace of mind to know that you and your family are prepared for the worst.

In this book, I have provided suggestions for preparedness. Ultimately, everybody's disaster preparedness is going to be different. Your living situation, where you live in the country, the types of natural disasters you are subject to, and your overall comfort level impact your preparedness. Using the guidelines presented in this book should help you put together the disaster preparedness plan that makes the most sense for you and your family. Preparedness is not a "one size fits all" solution. No two people put together the exact same Go Bag, for example. Take the information presented in this book and make it your own. Modify the lists as you see fit since only you know your life and your family. The most important thing is that you are planning. Any plan is better than no plan. Forewarned is forearmed or to put it another way: if you **are** ready, then you don't have to **get** ready.

Checklists

Over the course of this book, I presented quite a bit of information in lists with descriptions. Here I will present the lists without the extra descriptive information so you can use these as a checklist.

Family Emergency Communication Plan

This is used to provide you and all of your family the information to contact each other in the case of a disaster. While an electronic copy is good to have, you should have a hard copy as well.

For every member of your household:

- Full name
- Cell phone number
- Alternate phone number (landline, office, school)
- Email address
- Alternate email address
- Social media information (Facebook, Instagram, Twitter, WhatsApp)

For all utilities:

- Utility type (gas, water, electric, Internet, cell phone, etc.)
- 24-hour contact number
- Account number

For insurance:

- Insurance company
- 24-hour contact number
- Local agent's name
- Local agent's office address
- Local agent's phone number
- Policy number

Important Documents

These are important documents that allow you to establish your identification as well as other documents that you should have with you. Some of these are difficult to replace if they are damaged or lost.

To establish ID:

- Driver's license or state issued ID card
- Social Security card
- Passport
- Birth certificate or certificate of naturalization
- Permanent resident card ("Green Card")
- Military ID

Secondary sources of ID:

- Marriage license
- Divorce decree
- Child custody paperwork
- Employer (or school) ID card
- Voter registration card
- Automotive insurance card
- Vehicle registration
- Vehicle title
- Health insurance card
- Library card
- Amateur radio license
- Pilot's license
- Concealed firearm permit
- Deed of ownership of property
- W-2 Wage and Tax Statement

Other important documents:

- Copy of each utility bill
- Insurance policies (vehicle, homeowner's, renter's, etc.)
- Investment records
- Income Tax information (previous year's tax paperwork)
- Pay stub
- Employer benefit paperwork
- Medicare/Medicaid paperwork
- VA Health benefit paperwork
- Last Will and Testament
- Living Will

- Letter of Intent/Letter of Instruction
- Financial and medical powers of attorney
- Office information for family doctor, dentist, pediatrician, and any other specialists
- List of all prescription medication—including prescribing doctor and pharmacy
- Up-to-date immunization records
- Information on any allergies you have or medical equipment/devices you need
- Disability documentation
- Contact information for:
    - ◊ Employers
    - ◊ Schools
    - ◊ Local house of worship
    - ◊ Social service providers
    - ◊ Homeowners Association
    - ◊ List of trusted home repair services

For Pet Owners:

- Pet adoption information
- Registration information
- Vaccination records
- Any required tags (dogs tags, rabies vaccination tag, etc.)
- Microchip information
- A picture of you and your pet together
- Veterinarian contact information

Disaster Preparedness Kit for Your House

These items should be in your disaster preparedness kit for events of service interruptions lasting up to three days.

- A copy of all of your important documents
- Radio with NOAA band
- Flashlights
- Batteries
- First aid kit
- Face covering
- Tarps/plastic sheeting
- Duct tape
- Moist towelettes
- Garbage bags

- Plastic zip-ties
- Multitool
- Utility shut-off tool
- Manual can opener
- Battery packs for cell phones
- Blankets
- Rain poncho
- Pen and paper
- Heat source
- Books/magazines
- Pet supplies

Disaster Preparedness Kit for Your House—Phase 2

These items should be in your disaster preparedness kit for events or service interruptions lasting up to two weeks.

- A copy of all of your important documents
- Radio with NOAA band, multiple power sources
- Flashlights
- LED lanterns
- Batteries
- First aid kit, which includes at minimum
    - ◊ 2 absorbent compress dressings (5" × 9")
    - ◊ 25 adhesive bandages of assorted sizes
    - ◊ 5 packets of antibiotic ointment
    - ◊ 5 packets of antiseptic wipes
    - ◊ 2 packets of aspirin
    - ◊ 1 emergency blanket
    - ◊ 1 instant cold compress
    - ◊ 2 pairs of nonlatex gloves
    - ◊ 2 packets of hydrocortisone ointment
    - ◊ 1 roll of 3" gauze bandage
    - ◊ 1 roll of 4" bandage
    - ◊ 5 sterile pads (3" × 3")
    - ◊ 5 sterile gauze pads (4" × 4")
    - ◊ 1 thermometer—oral, non-mercury, non-glass
    - ◊ 2 triangular bandages
    - ◊ 1 pair of tweezers
- Signal whistle and/or signal mirror

- Face covering
- Tarps/plastic sheeting
- Moist towelettes
- Toiletries (toothpaste, toothbrush, deodorant, etc.)
- Feminine hygiene products
- Garbage bags
- Plastic zip-ties
- Multitool
- Utility shut-off tool
- Manual can opener
- Battery packs for cell phone
- Blankets
- Sleeping bag
- Complete change of clothing (weather appropriate)
- Rain poncho
- Boots
- Work gloves
- Pen and paper
- Paper map of the local area
- 30-day supply of prescription medication
- Over-the-counter (OTC) medication
    - ◊ Aspirin
    - ◊ Ibuprofen
    - ◊ Antacids
    - ◊ Antihistamines
    - ◊ Bismuth subsalicylate
    - ◊ Cough medicine
    - ◊ Laxatives
    - ◊ Sleep aids
    - ◊ Saline spray
    - ◊ Vitamins
    - ◊ Cash
    - ◊ Paper plates/plastic utensils
    - ◊ Books/magazines/games
    - ◊ Pet supplies

Disaster Preparedness Kit for Your House—Phase 3

These items should be in your disaster preparedness kit for events or service interruptions lasting several weeks.

- A copy of all of your important documents
- Radios with NOAA band and multiple power sources—at least 2
- Flashlights—several
- LED lanterns—several
- Batteries
- First aid kit, custom built to include:
    - ◊ Tweezers
    - ◊ Non-contact thermometer
    - ◊ Cotton swabs
    - ◊ Trauma shears
    - ◊ Surgical-grade toenail clippers
    - ◊ Disposable scalpel
    - ◊ Stethoscope
    - ◊ Suture kit
    - ◊ Blister treatment
    - ◊ Irrigation syringe
    - ◊ Absorbent compress dressings (5" × 9")
    - ◊ Adhesive bandages (assorted sizes)
    - ◊ Sterile gauze pads
    - ◊ Antiseptic wipes
    - ◊ Emergency blanket
    - ◊ Ace bandage
    - ◊ Triangle bandages
    - ◊ Tegaderm bandages
    - ◊ Butterfly bandages—aka "steri-strips"
    - ◊ SAM splint
    - ◊ Israeli bandage
    - ◊ Tourniquet
    - ◊ Chest seal
    - ◊ Non-latex gloves–1 box
    - ◊ Instant cold compress
    - ◊ Clotting agents
    - ◊ Permanent marker
    - ◊ Small flashlight
- 30-day supply of prescription medication
- Over-the counter (OTC) medication
    - ◊ Aspirin
    - ◊ Ibuprofen
    - ◊ Antacids
    - ◊ Antihistamines
    - ◊ Bismuth subsalicylate

    - ◊ Cough medicine
    - ◊ Pseudoephedrine
    - ◊ Throat lozenges
    - ◊ Oral rehydration
    - ◊ Laxatives
    - ◊ Sleep aids
    - ◊ Cranberry extract
    - ◊ Saline spray
    - ◊ Vitamins
    - ◊ Antibiotic ointment
    - ◊ Hydrocortisone cream
    - ◊ Miconazole cream
    - ◊ Antibacterial soap
- Signal whistle
- Signal mirror
- Lumber—planks and full 4 × 8 sheets
- Hammer and nails
- Tarps
- Plastic sheets
- Duct tape
- Plastic zip-ties
- Face covering
- Moist towelettes
- Toiletries
- Feminine hygiene products
- Garbage bags
- Multitool
- Utility shut-off tool
- Manual can opener
- Battery packs for cell phones
- Blankets
- Sleeping bags
- Complete change of clothes (weather appropriate)
- Rain poncho
- Boots
- Work gloves
- Pen and paper
- Paper map of the local area
- Cash
- Paper plates and plastic utensils
- Books/magazines/games
- Pet supplies

- Sufficient food and water
- 30 days' worth of any prescription medications
- Other medications (heartworm, flea and tick, etc.)
- Shelter
- Treats and toys
- Extra leash and collar (with ID tag)
- Pet first aid kit
- Roll of cotton bandage
- Roll of bandage tape
- Scissors
- Antibiotic ointment
- Non-latex gloves
- Saline solution
- Isopropyl alcohol
- Pet first aid guide

Get Home Bag

Kept in your car or at work, a Get Home Bag has everything you need to get back home safely.

- Backpack
- Water bottle
- Sillcock key
- Food–1 day's worth
- Headlamp
- Rain poncho
- Tarp
- First aid kit
- Multitool
- Paracord
- Duct tape
- Paper map of the local area
- Compass
- Pen and paper
- Signal whistle
- Signal mirror
- Face covering
- Eye protection
- Hat
- Gloves

- Hand warmers
- Complete change of clothes (weather appropriate)
- Durable walking shoes
- Emergency radio with NOAA band
- Personal protection
- Cash

Go Bag

A Go Bag is used when you need to quickly evacuate your house and you expect to be gone for up to three days.

- Backpack
- Emergency contact list
- Copy of your important documents
- Water bottle
- Water purification and/or sillcock key
- 3 days' worth of emergency rations
- Radio with NOAA band
- Battery pack for cell phone
- First aid kit including
  - ◊ Adhesive bandages
  - ◊ Non-latex gloves
  - ◊ Gauze pads–2" × 2" and 4" × 4"
  - ◊ Butterfly bandages—aka "steri-strips"
  - ◊ Triangular bandage
  - ◊ Hemostatic agent
  - ◊ Self-adhesive bandage
  - ◊ Rolled gauze
  - ◊ Israeli bandage
  - ◊ Tourniquet
  - ◊ Chest seal
  - ◊ SAM splint
  - ◊ Antibiotic cream
  - ◊ Burn pads
  - ◊ Moleskin pads
  - ◊ Antibacterial wet wipes
  - ◊ Eye drops
  - ◊ Sunscreen
  - ◊ Anesthetic swabs
  - ◊ Over-the-counter medication

    - ◊ Aspirin
    - ◊ Acetaminophen
    - ◊ Ibuprofen
    - ◊ Antacid tablets
    - ◊ Prescription medication—three days' worth
    - ◊ Medical shears
    - ◊ Tweezers
    - ◊ Safety pins
- Flashlight or headlamp
- Chemlights
- Emergency blanket
- Pen and paper
- Paper map of the local area
- Compass
- Signal whistle
- Signal mirror
- Toiletries
- Complete change of clothing (weather appropriate)
- Face covering
- Eye protection
- Gloves
- Cash
- Multitool
- Paracord
- Duct tape
- Trash bags
- Tarp
- Sewing kit
- Hand warmers
- Fire starter
- Personal protection
- Entertainment
- Pet supplies
    - ◊ Food
    - ◊ Portable water bowl
    - ◊ Leash
    - ◊ Collar with ID tag

Index